Improving Conference Design and Outcomes

Paul J. Ilsley, *Editor*

NEW DIRECTIONS FOR CONTINUING EDUCATION
GORDON G. DARKENWALD, *Editor-in-Chief*
ALAN B. KNOX, Consulting Editor

Number 28, December 1985

Paperback sourcebooks in
The Jossey-Bass Higher Education Series

Jossey-Bass Inc., Publishers
San Francisco • London

Paul J. Ilsley (Ed.).
Improving Conference Design and Outcomes.
New Directions for Continuing Education, no. 28.
San Francisco: Jossey-Bass, 1985.

New Directions for Continuing Education
Gordon G. Darkenwald, *Editor-in-Chief*
Alan B. Knox, *Consulting Editor*

New Directions for Continuing Education (publication number
USPS 493-930) is published quarterly by Jossey-Bass Inc., Publishers.
Second class postage rates paid at San Francisco, California,
and at additional mailing offices.

Correspondence:
Subscriptions, single-issue orders, change of address notices,
undelivered copies, and other correspondence should be sent
to Subscriptions, Jossey-Bass Inc., Publishers, 433 California Street,
San Francisco, California 94104.

Editorial correspondence should be sent to the managing
Editor-in-Chief, Gordon G. Darkenwald, Graduate School
of Education, Rutgers University, 10 Seminary Place, New
Brunswick, New Jersey 08903.

Library of Congress Catalogue Card Number LC 85-60829
International Standard Serial Number ISSN 0195-2242
International Standard Book Number ISBN 87589-746-0

Cover art by WILLI BAUM
Manufactured in the United States of America

Ordering Information

The paperback sourcebooks listed below are published quarterly and can be ordered either by subscription or single-copy.

Subscriptions cost $40.00 per year for institutions, agencies, and libraries. Individuals can subscribe at the special rate of $30.00 per year *if payment is by personal check*. (Note that the full rate of $40.00 applies if payment is by institutional check, even if the subscription is designated for an individual.) Standing orders are accepted.

Single copies are available at $9.95 when payment accompanies order, and *all single-copy orders under $25.00 must include payment*. (California, New Jersey, New York, and Washington, D.C., residents please include appropriate sales tax.) For billed orders, cost per copy is $9.95 plus postage and handling. (Prices subject to change without notice.)

Bulk orders (ten or more copies) of any individual sourcebook are available at the following discounted prices: 10–49 copies, $8.95 each; 50–100 copies, $7.96 each; over 100 copies, *inquire*. Sales tax and postage and handling charges apply as for single copy orders.

To ensure correct and prompt delivery, all orders must give either the *name of an individual* or an *official purchase order number*. Please submit your order as follows:

Subscriptions: specify series and year subscription is to begin.
Single Copies: specify sourcebook code (such as, CE1) and first two words of title.

Mail orders for United States and Possessions, Latin America, Canada, Japan, Australia, and New Zealand to:
    Jossey-Bass Inc., Publishers
    433 California Street
    San Francisco, California 94104

Mail orders for all other parts of the world to:
    Jossey-Bass Limited
    28 Banner Street
    London EC1Y 8QE

New Directions for Continuing Education Series
Gordon G. Darkenwald, *Editor-in-Chief*
Alan B. Knox, *Consulting Editor*

Contents

Editor's Notes

What are some of the key strategies that planners must keep in mind in order to achieve a successful conference? How do some conference participants learn to maximize the conference experience? To address these questions, this sourcebook takes a three-part approach. The first section is devoted to planning strategies for conferences, expecially large conferences with more than a thousand. The authors use true-to-life examples of conference planning situations to illustrate principles. The three chapters in this section present the respective themes of developing a planning process (Cope, Chapter One), anticipating pitfalls (Ratcliff, Chapter Two), and establishing optimal environmental conditions (Foucar-Szocki, Chapter Three). In short, these chapters address the issue of creating a conference, and they pay special attention to aspects that are usually taken for granted, such as organization, teamwork, decor, and ambience.

The second section treats the topic of conference participation, emphasizing how participants can maximize the conference experience for career and personal growth. Novel implications of a consumer viewpoint are presented for planners from the perspectives of both newcomers and experienced participants. The first chapter in this section identifies barriers to full conference participation and presents guidelines for tailoring involvement (through the making of wise choices) to fit personal and professional goals (Boucouvalas, Chapter Four). The second chapter analyzes the special problems facing first-time participants, such as feelings of exclusion, and it outlines strategies for increasing their levels of involvement (Meyer, Chapter Five).

The third section offers provocative and practical considerations regarding ideal conferences. One chapter (Collins, Chapter Six) challenges readers to consider the proposition that residential conferences offer advantages over huge conventions in terms of quality of interaction and learning. Another chapter (Draves, Chapter Seven) treats the theme of trends in conference design by reminding planners and consumers alike that many tendencies of the past are likely to continue into the future; however, participants are likely to become more selective about conference attendance. The last chapter (Ilsley, Chapter Eight) pulls together themes of successful conference planning and participation and reviews the literature base for readers who wish to inquire further. In short, this sourcebook provides both conference planners and consumers with a realistic perspective regarding the purposes, design, and limits of conferences.

Paul J. Ilsley
Editor

Paul J. Ilsley is assistant professor of adult education at Syracuse University. He is coauthor of Recruiting and Training Volunteers, *and he has spent eleven years planning and consuming conferences.*

Successful conference planning begins with a well-organized plan.

Developing a Planning Process for Large Conferences

Judith L. Cope

During this period of austerity and budget cutting, there is a sensitivity toward conference time and costs. A poor conference may shatter the morale of attendees, who go away feeling that their association does not care about them or, worse, that it is incompetent. Most association-type conferences are primarily planned, managed, and evaluated by volunteers. Without volunteers, large conferences would not exist. However, not all volunteers are skilled in conference planning. Some come to the experience with an extensive and varied background, while others are well meaning but short on know-how and experience, as Meyer points out in Chapter Five.

There is little written information that can assist conference planners, particularly those who have responsibility for large conferences. Developing clear written policies and procedures on the conduct of large conferences would improve the quality. Such procedures could help conference planners to plan more efficiently and systematically. As a step in that direction, this chapter outlines major aspects of the planning of large conferences. These major aspects are a well-planned and well-structured organizational system and a detailed budget. Although conferences sponsored by voluntary associations are emphasized, many of the same principles apply to other types of large conferences.

P. J. Ilsley (Ed.). *Improving Conference Design and Outcomes.* New Directions for Continuing Education, no. 28. San Francisco: Jossey-Bass, December 1985.

The Organizational System

General Chairperson. The general chairperson of a conference plays a major role in its success or failure. The chairperson is instrumental in establishing an organizational structure appropriate to the local political, social, and fiscal climate. Figure 1 depicts the structure of a large conference planning committee in a graphic way. The chart reflects lines of authority, reporting relationships, and levels of responsibility. The organizational hierarchy can be structured in such a way as to promote two-way communication between the chairperson and the program coordinators. The chart is traditional in that it depicts the lines of authority and the flow of descending hierarchy. The general chairperson carries the ultimate responsibility but also reports to the paid staff (if an association is working with the conference) and to elected officials (if it is an association conference)—the board of directors. The farther down a position is on the chart, the greater is the diffusion of responsibility. A large conference does not take place without a combined effort of volunteers dedicated and committed toward common goals. This dedication should be strong enough that each volunteer has a stake in the success of the conference. It is the role of the general chairperson and the coordinators to exhibit leadership with their committees by proceeding as a unit of one in the spirit of colleagueship and dedication to the achievements of conference goals.

The chart depicted in Figure 1 is not the be-all and end-all. It is simply a tried and proved organizational system that has been used successfully for the planning and implementing of large association-type conferences. Certainly it can be modified to suit the size of the conference, the sponsoring organization, and the fiscal and human resource constraints. The terms *coordinator* and *chairperson* can be used interchangeably for smaller conferences with fewer volunteers. The roots of the chart depicted in Figure 1 are documented in the closing report of the National Adult Education Conference (Smith, 1980).

Executive Committee. The executive committee is headed by the general chairperson of the conference. The general chairperson should possess leadership skills, be capable of formulating the conceptual framework of the conference, be compatible with committee members, and possess the ability to work as a team member. In the context of a conference, the leader is a person who understands human behavior and who can motivate people. A good conference leader is not only aware of the planners' personal goals and objectives but especially sensitive and responsive to their genuine wants and needs.

The general chairperson selects and appoints the executive committee members. Members should be dependable, skillful, reliable, and honest and they should have access to the support services needed to accomplish committee activities. The members of the executive committee

Figure 1. Illustrative Organization Chart

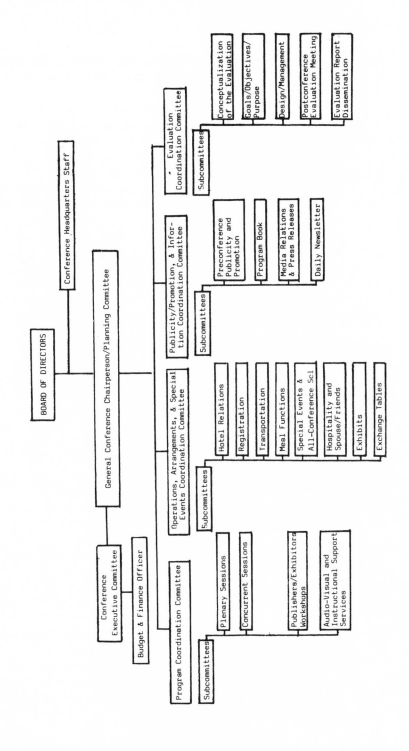

help to establish, review, or approve the conference goals, the conference theme and logo, the organizational structure used for planning the conference, the conference planning action plan and time schedule, the conference budget, the conference evaluation, and the conference program schedule. (See Figure 2.)

Figure 2. Overall Action Plan and Time Schedule

Prior to conference:

6 years	1.	Establish site selection committee
5 years	2.	Ratify site and conference dates
2 years	3.	Appoint conference chairperson
22 months	4.	Appoint committee chairs, executive committee, and fiscal officer.
20 months	5.	Conduct initial executive committee meeting
19 months	6.	Conduct second executive committee meeting
18 months	7.	Schedule executive committee meetings to plan for promotional activities (booth and reception) at prior conference
13 months	8.	Complete pre-year conference brochure
13 months	9.	Complete the progress report
12 months	10.	Present progress report to board of directors
12 months	11.	Attend post-conference evaluation meeting at prior conference
11 months	12.	Print conference stationery
10 months	13.	Mail out call for presenters
9 months	14.	Mail out first conference brochure
6 months	15.	Mail out final conference brochure
3 months	16.	Complete the program book
2 months	17.	Complete conference staff schedules
1 month	18.	Review conference staff schedule
1 week	19.	Conduct all-conference planning check
Day Before	20.	Train conference staff
First Day/ 7:00 a.m.	21.	Conference staff report for work

After conference:

1 month	22.	Complete and distribute conference evaluation report
2 months	23	Close fiscal books
3 months	24.	Complete and distribute final conference report

The plan and time schedule in Figure 2 evolved from National Adult Education Conference experiences and reports documented from 1977 to 1983. (Standing Service Unit on National Conferences, 1983)

The general chairperson monitors the executive committee and conference committees and is ultimately responsible for overall conference planning, implementation, and evaluation. In addition, the chairperson writes the final conference report and sends thank-you letters and certificates of appreciation to conference planners and presenters after the conference.

The general chairperson serves as the motivator, initiator, and innovator to encourage committee members to feel a sense of ownership of the conference through participation in the planning process.

The logistics of executive committee meetings are extremely important. An agenda and minutes should be kept at each meeting in order to maintain accurate records for decision making and action that needs to be taken. It is necessary to establish clear-cut purposes, objectives, well-ordered plans, and a time schedule.

The executive committee members provide the conference planning process with its foundation. While the work of this committee often seems to be mundane, the decisions that it makes provide the necessary basis for the implementation of a successful conference.

Program Committee. The coordinator of the program committee, like other coordinators, should be a leader. This person should understand the conference goals, theme, and priorities; be compatible with the subcommittee members; and possess the ability to work as a team member. Even more important, this individual should have staff development, in-service, or program or conference experience and possess an in-depth understanding of all the responsibilities of program subcommittees. In addition to these skills, the program coordinator needs to have some released time from regular work assignments and access to support services, such as telephone, postage, and secretarial assistance, in order to accomplish the tasks necessary to develop the conference program successfully. This committee prepares and disseminates the call for papers; plans plenary sessions, concurrent sessions, and preconference workshops; and arranges for audiovisual support services. The program committee contributes the majority of the information for the conference program book. The program committee coordinator is a member of the executive committee and reports on program activities at executive committee meetings.

Plenary Sessions Subcommittee. The assignment for the plenary sessions subcommittee is to identify dynamic general session speakers who will help to sell the conference and increase attendance. These speakers must at the same time address the concerns of the membership as they relate to the conference's theme and goals. The assignment is difficult when there are severe budget constraints. Nevertheless, subcommittee members present a ranked list of potential speakers with biographical information (and photos if available), together with information about topic and cost to the program coordinator, who in turn transmits the information to the executive committee for final approval. After the selection is made, the subcommittee then prepares and submits public relations packages to appropriate committees regarding the speakers. Backup general session speakers should be identified in case of an unforeseen emergency.

Concurrent Sessions Subcommittee. The concurrent sessions subcommittee is central to the success of a conference. Its major role is to arrange high-quality sessions, to identify speakers whose track record is known in the field and whose presentations can help to develop the theme and integrate it into the conference program. It also schedules concurrent sessions. This subcommittee keeps the communication lines open with the program coordinator, who reports to the executive committee. One of its first responsibilities is to prepare and disseminate the call for papers. After the paper proposals have been received, the subcommittee screens them against predetermined criteria, makes a selection, and schedules them for presentation. Screening and scheduling can take between six and eight months. It is recommended that the association leadership take an active role in screening the proposals submitted for consideration. The conference program should reflect the broad range of the membership's interests and concerns. Scheduling is critical. There should be no conflicts between sessions on the same topic, business meetings, other major conference activities, association activities, or social events.

Some planners prefer to schedule no evening sessions since they are often not well attended; however, it is recommended that special meetings be held in the evenings. This subcommittee must schedule, approve, and confirm the day, time, room number, room capacity, estimated attendance, room arrangements, and needed audiovisual equipment. It provides the majority of the program information in the program book committee, and it works closely with the local operations and arrangements committee to ensure that its requests are carried out.

Special Sessions Subcommittee. The special sessions subcommittee is responsible for such sessions as newcomer's orientation. Group activities, such as the Juntos organized at the American Association for Adult and Continuing Education (AAACE) national adult education conference in Philadelphia in 1983, provide participants with opportunities to discuss critical professional issues. The AAACE used ongoing discussions patterned after Ben Franklin's famous Junto, which still exists in Philadelphia to give special attention to selected issues. This subcommittee's other responsibilities include making arrangements for publishers, exhibitors, and preconference workshops. The subcommittee schedules these sessions by day, date, and time and reviews them for conflicts with the conference schedule. These sessions also help to develop the theme and facilitate its integration into the conference program.

Audiovisual Support Services Subcommittee. The audiovisual support services subcommittee identifies all the audiovisual equipment needs, determines the source of equipment support services, monitors the audiovisual and support system during the conference, and handles audiovisual emergencies, such as burned-out bulbs, equipment breakdowns, and the like.

Operations and Arrangements Committee. The coordinator of the operations and arrangements committee is the ambassador of goodwill for the executive committee and other conference planners. The operations and arrangements committee develops and nurtures hotel relations; establishes formal registration procedures; arranges for meal functions; plans special events and the all-conference social; arranges the hospitality activities for spouses, family, and friends; and coordinates the exchange tables and transportation, including special airline schedules or limousines and buses. To work effectively with the hotel representatives, the committee's coordinator must have excellent interpersonal, political, and diplomatic skills. Released time and support services, such as telephone, postage, and secretarial help, are prerequisites for the person who assumes these responsibilities. Satisfactory hotel relations and conference operations must be coordinated. Working with the general chairpersons, the operations and arrangements committee coordinator develops a detailed budget that realistically reflects the expected revenues and expenditures for the functions of the committee. The coordinator is the monitor of fiscal matters related to committee activities. Of course, the operations and arrangements coordinator is a member of the executive committee and therefore is prepared to make periodic reports about all operations, arrangements, and special events. One way to smooth the functioning of an operations and arrangements committee is to establish subcommittees. The next seven paragraphs describe some typical subcommittees.

Hotel Relations Subcommittee. The responsibility of the hotel relations subcommittee is to meet with the designated hotel convention coordinator in order to arrange all provisions of the contract. The chairperson of the hotel relations subcommittee becomes the official contact with hotel staff, because the committee is responsible for sleeping rooms, reservations, guest room rates, meeting room policies, food and meal arrangements, and rental fees. Thus, the chairperson of this subcommittee is in a key position to monitor hotel overflow accommodations, reserve conference rooms on an emergency basis, inspect a daily accounting of hotel room usage, and arrange for parking information. The program coordinator works closely with the hotel relations chairperson in order to coordinate the meeting rooms with program events. It is the hotel relations chairperson who reviews the final hotel bill with the general conference chairperson and arranges for payment of the bill in conjunction with the fiscal officer. The hotel relations subcommittee chairperson collects and submits all hotel bills to the fiscal officer, who reviews and files them for use by future conference budget planners.

Registration Subcommittee. It is the responsibility of the chairperson of the registration subcommittee to recommend fees for registration, special events, and meal functions. The subcommittee chair and members of the subcommittee work closely with the national headquarters to keep an accurate account of registrants, meal tickets, special events, and membership dues as they are received. The registration subcommittee members also work closely with the individuals who are responsible for the program book.

It is the responsibility of the registration subcommittee to develop formal registration procedures. The registration area at a conference is the place where participants first gather and where the general ambience of the conference is established. Ideally, registration volunteers are dependable as well as cheerful and helpful. On-site registration procedures need to be reviewed one to two days before the conference starts. Volunteers should receive written guidelines and simulation practice in advance of the conference. The written materials can include a description of the conference stations, a floor plan showing the location of conference stations, a list of participants with sample materials, a list of necessary audiovisual equipment, a list of registration instructions, and examples of what to do when problems occur, such as lost receipts or lost lunch tickets. Other special services that might be offered at the registration area are a bank service, information about nearby restaurants and maps and lists of special events and activities available in the conference locality. It is the responsibility of the registration committee chairperson—indeed, it is the responsibility of all chairpersons—to collect and maintain all documents pertaining to the subcommittee's activities so that they can be included in the final report and filed with the sponsoring organization for use by future conference planners. (Copeland, 1983.)

Meal Function Subcommittee. The meal functions subcommittee coordinates all meal functions, obtains the policy for meal functions, and duplicates selected breakfast, lunch, and dinner menus for distribution to groups requesting meal functions with major meetings. This subcommittee maintains an accurate account of meal function requests and coordinates scheduling for the meals; informs the hotel of the final estimate of guaranteed meals to be served under the deadlines established by the hotel contract; confirms requested meal functions in writing, investigates all rules and regulations concerning food at the hotel; arranges all coffee breaks and cash bars, fast food, and quick breakfasts; and confirms complimentary meal policy with the sponsoring agency.

Special Events and All-Conference Social Subcommittee. The primary tasks of the special events and all-conference social subcommittee are to plan the opening session, the grand opening of the exhibits, and the all-conference social event, which is an opportunity for participants to meet one another on an informal basis. Spouses, family, and friends, of course, are also invited. Music, dancing, and games may be included. The other responsibilities of this subcommittee are to determine the types of functions that will attract the majority of attendees, determine what expenses are reasonable, seek under-writing for the social event from a publishing company or other corporation, and recommend budgetary needs to the operations and arrangements committee coordinator for approval by the executive committee. The chairperson of this subcommittee monitors all fiscal transactions to be sure that they remain within the guidelines of the proposed special event budget. The subcommittee determines appropriate themes for socials. The all-conference social should take place at the conference site or at a reasonably convenient and accessible distance from that site. This subcommittee also coordinates awards ceremonies. It should arrange for music and any special activities throughout the conference, including the opening session and the grand opening of the exhibits, and it should provide visibility for the conference within the community by such means as billboards, electric marquees, and other mass media strategies.

Hospitality for Spouses, Family, and Friends Subcommittee. The task of the hospitality for spouses, family, and friends subcommittee is to select committee members to represent various groups and organizations, such as universities, colleges, public schools, hospitals, prisons, and business and industry, from the host city and from across the host state. Together these individuals can arrange tours, visits, special parties, educational activities, and pre- and postconference tours, and they can provide publicity via brochures, pamphlets, and fliers. It is helpful to arrange for a hospitality room or booth, and to have subcommittee members act as hosts or hostesses for speakers, important guests, and celebrities. The members of this subcommittee should work closely with the program committee.

Transportation Subcommittee. The chairperson of the transportation subcommittee is responsible for arranging special airline discount rates for members who wish to attend the conference and for arranging car rental discounts. The transportation subcommittee can also establish a welcome booth at the airport.

Exhibits Subcommittee. Exhibits are important to a conference. For one thing, they keep participants informed about the latest resources. For another, they generate revenue. The exhibit subcommittee is responsible for preregistration forms and the exhibit brochure. Exhibit information is sent to past and prospective exhibitors, the hotel exhibit manager, and decorating and drayage firms. The exhibit manager recruits local volunteers to help in the exhibit area during the conference. The exhibit manager develops a time schedule to design, print, and mail a cover letter and the exhibit brochure; sets deadlines to negotiate contracts; and collects exhibit fees. Contracts are negotiated with decorator and drayage firms. Floor plans are drawn up by the hotel to show various space layouts. The exhibit manager determines the best location for exhibit functions and such activities as exchange tables, coffee service, drawings, and hospitality. The floor plan is included in the exhibitor's brochure. Finally, the exhibit manager completes the contracts and keeps careful records about the resulting arrangements. During the conference, the exhibits subcommittee provides services to exhibitors, such as security guards, coffee, and additional decorator or drayage services. After the conference, the exhibit manager sends thank-you letters to the exhibitors and prepares a final report with recommendations for the next year.

Promotion, Publicity, and Information Committee. The coordinator of the promotion, publicity, and information committee is crucial to the success of a conference. The coordinator can substantially increase conference attendance, improve the sponsoring organization's image, and increase the visibility of the conference. The coordinator should possess professional public relations and marketing skills. The coordinator researches and compiles mailing lists, then markets the lists according to a well-thought-out plan. The coordinator is a member of the executive committee. He or she acts as liaison between the general conference chairperson and the conference coordinators and reports on such matters as promotion, publicity, and conference information at executive meetings. The promotion, publicity, and information committee prepares and disseminates the preconference publicity and promotion and the conference program book, arranges media relations and press releases, and provides input for the daily newsletter.

Preconference Publicity Subcommittee. The preconference publicity subcommittee recommends a conference logo to be used on all stationery and printed materials to the executive committee. It prepares professional, first-class, stimulating copy that can promote attendance at the conference. This copy emphasizes exceptional and unique features of the program that can be used to promote speakers, facilities, city, or site. Another responsibility of this subcommittee is to prepare preconference brochures for membership registration and program information. The preconference material includes the very first fliers for promotional booth dissemination and reception circulated one year prior to the conference. These fliers use the conference theme, logo, and colors. The subcommittee also prepares and disseminates conference stationery. It mails out the tickler copy to the membership. The tickler copy identifies the conference theme and confirms the speakers and the dates for special events and sessions. This subcommittee facilitates the dissemination of program information from the program and arrangements coordinators and it obtains mailing lists and distributes information from and to other related professional organizations. The chairperson of this committee writes conference features and display ads for educational journals. Other publicity products that can be developed are placemats, posters, presenter and volunteer appreciation certificates, buttons, press cards, signs, banners, pens, and various customized conference products. The members of this subcommittee should work closely with the operations and arrangements committee and the special events subcommittee. Finally, this subcommittee collaborates with the registration subcommittee and other pertinent committees to collect information for preconference publicity.

Program Book Subcommittee. The chairperson of the program book subcommittee works closely with the executive committee, the printer, and the graphic artist to plan the contents and layout of the program book. The members of this subcommittee work closely with national headquarters staff to negotiate paid advertisements with publishing companies, restaurants, and other businesses. The program book should incorporate the official theme, logo, and colors into its design. Pictures of significant presenters, leaders, and guests should be included. The members of this subcommittee edit and proofread the content of the books to ensure that it is accurate and consistent. Large print and well-indexed books are preferred. A three-ring notebook-style format can be recommended, because it allows participants to add extra pages.

Media and Press Releases Subcommittee. The media and press releases subcommittee plays a critical role in conference activities, but its work is often neglected. Its functions are to operate and staff a newsroom at the conference site for six hours a day. The conference headquarters often doubles as the newsroom. Official conference stationery, duplication service, and typewriters should be available at this location. Appointments with local and national radio, television, and press representatives are scheduled in the newsroom or conference headquarters. Press kits, including a program book, are made available to general mass media and educational writers. Photographs are made available, and media photographers are provided assistance in photographing major sessions, the registration area, exhibits, and selected sessions.

Daily Newsletters Subcommittee. The daily newsletters subcommittee prepares the daily newsletter to announce updates, revisions, and changes in the program. Hotel television monitors may provide an alternative to a daily newsletter. The newsletter uses the conference theme, logo, and colors. The members of this subcommittee will also arrange for typing and duplication services and create a distribution plan for the daily newsletter.

Evaluation Committee. It is important for an association's members to know the strengths and weaknesses of its national conference. It is up to the evaluation coordinator to collect the necessary information. The evaluation coordinator collects information for two reasons: to improve decision making and to provide accountability. The evaluation coordinator helps the executive committee to establish conference goals and objectives. Evaluation activities should have a budget appropriate to carry out the evaluation activities requested by the executive committee and the general conference chairperson. The evaluation committee may then establish the goals, objectives, and purpose of the conference evaluation. The evaluation coordinator designs the evaluation plan, conducts a postconference evaluation meeting, and prepares and disseminates the final evaluation report. (Cope, 1981).

Goals, Objectives, and Purpose. In order to establish the goals, objectives, and purpose of the conference evaluation, the evaluation coordinator must work closely with the conference chairperson and the program coordinators to determine the evaluation needs of the conference. Once the needs have been established, they can be translated into evaluation questions. These questions should then be ratified by the executive committee. When the questions are ratified, the evaluation coordinator and evaluation committee members should review them to develop an evaluation design and establish the primary focus of the evaluation. It is incumbent on an evaluation coordinator to solicit evaluation questions related to the conference theme, goals, and primary focus of the conference. The use to which answers to each evaluation question will be put must be determined in advance. The information that is collected must be perceived as useful by conference planners for the purpose of evaluation.

Evaluation Design. The evaluation instruments and the management system should be designed around the evaluation questions. Information can be obtained through structured interviews (by telephone or mail), observation, public forums, surveys, and questionnaires. The possible audiences include conference planners, conference presenters, conference participants, association members, association committees, association commissions or sections, association staff, funding agencies, and content specialists. Development of the evaluation design should be budgeted. The management plan should address nine issues: conceptualization of the evaluation; channels that can influence policy and decision making; establishment of a policy to govern the evaluation; the evaluation staff; the equipment and materials needed; the data-gathering instruments; the reporting schedule; any evaluation training needed by staff, graduate students, and selected conference planners; and use of the findings. The management plan should be used as an outline to carry out the evaluation. Details should include how to organize the evaluation and how to type, print, and copy the evaluation forms.

Evaluation Report and Dissemination. A good evaluation report includes the following elements: title page, table of contents, preface, abstract, introduction, goals, objectives, procedures, analysis of data, summary, conclusions and recommendations, and appendixes. It should include information about committee composition, communication channels, past evaluation data, definition, purpose, policies, planning groups, evaluation design, budget, management plan, evaluators' orientation and training, and dissemination. Dissemination of the evaluation report to appropriate decision makers is one of the most critical steps in the evaluation process. The evaluation report should be completed approximately one month after the conference, and it should be made available to the planning group for the following year and to other appropriate decision makers at that time. It is recommended that the dissemination process be standardized and that recipients and the repository of evaluation information be identified before evaluation begins. For example: evaluation results can be published in an association journal.

The Detailed Budget

The detailed budget presented in this section has been constructed from logs and records for five years (1977–1981) of National Adult

Conferences. The percentages are derived from three years (1983–1985) of National Adult Education Conferences (Cope, 1984; Maloney, 1985; Robinson, 1985).

Overall Budget Concept. Well-planned budgets help to maximize attendance at the lowest possible cost. Conference planners should prepare two budgets: one for revenues and one for expenditures. The projected revenue budget is based on previous attendance and registration figures, special events and exhibit fees, and advertising revenues. The decision to determine the fees can be made jointly by the general conference chairperson, the association staff, the executive committee, and the fiscal officer. Records of past conferences addressing such issues as the effects of geographic location, registration patterns, and overhead costs, can be used with other data to set fees at the lowest rate possible that is still high enough to realize a profit. Likewise, conference planners should prepare a projected expenditures budget based on anticipated expenses. The geographic location will create other factors to consider, such as potential attendance and exhibit space costs. Obviously, by reducing overhead expenses, by increasing fees, or both, profits can be increased. Experience has shown that conference budget revenues are largely derived from registration fees, special events, meal functions, workshops, exhibits, and advertisement fees.

It is recommended that budget expenditures and revenues correspond to the functions depicted on the conference organization chart. This practice provides the general conference chairperson, executive committee, and committee coordinators with an easily understood budget structure. The illustrative budget included in this section is based on the organization chart depicted in Figure 1.

Revenues

R1	Conference registration	65%
R2	Special events and meal functions	13%
R3	Workshops, exhibits, advertisements	22%
	Total	100%

Expenditures

E1	Program committee	13%
E2	Operations and arrangement committee	34%
E3	Publicity, promotion, and information committee	41%
E4	Executive Committee	3%
E5	Evaluation committee	1%
E6	Staff travel expenses	6%
E7	Contingency expenses	2%
	Total	100%

Conference Revenues. The purpose of promoting a large conference is to increase the number of registrations. Registrations alone bring in approximately 65 percent of conference revenues. While there are no scientific rules to help conference planners maximize revenue, it is obvious that a great deal of attention must be paid to the establishment of fees and promotional activities. The revenues for registration can be considered in the following way:

    R1   Conference registration (65%)

        1.1 National members preregistration

        1.2 Local members preregistration

        1.3 On-site member registration

        1.4 On-site nonmember registration

        1.5 Retirees and students registration

        1.6 One-day registration

The goals and benefits of special events and meal functions should be vigorously promoted, since it is estimated that they generate approximately 13 percent of the revenues. The revenues from special events and meal functions can be illustrated in the following manner:

    R2   Special events/meal functions (13%)

        2.1 Awards and fellowship luncheon

        2.2 Special luncheons

        2.3 Special dinners

        2.4 All-conference social

        2.5 Side tours

The preconference workshops, exhibits, and advertisements are the second biggest money maker for a conference, since they raise about 22 percent of its revenue budget. The preconference workshops and arrangements for the audiovisual equipment are made by the program committee. Arrangements for program book advertisements are planned by the publicity, promotion, and information committee. Exhibits are coordinated by operations and arrangements committee. Contributions are made primarily to assist with association functions at the conference. The breakdown for other revenue is estimated as follows:

    R3   Workshops, exhibits, and advertisements (22%)

        3.1 Exhibits

        3.2 Preconference workshops

        3.3 Program book advertisements

        3.4 Audiovisual Equipment

        3.5 Contributions to underwrite special events, receptions, and/or marketing

Conference Expenditures. It is recommended that the conference organization chart proposed in this chapter should be used to structure the budget plan for expenditures. Each category of the budget for expenditures can be planned in conjunction with the general conference chairperson, headquarters staff, and the appropriate committee coordinators. After the association board has approved the budget, the coordinators are expected to carry out their conference-planning activities within the budget allocations. In order to change or modify budget allocations, each coordinator must have prior approval by three gatekeepers: the conference general chairperson, conference headquarters staff liaison, and the fiscal officer. Here are some illustrative expenditure categories:

E 1   Program committee
E 2   Operations and arrangements committee
E 3   Publicity, promotion, and information committee
E 4   Executive committee
E 5   Evaluation committee
E 6   Staff travel expenses
E 7   Contingency expenses

Program Committee. The program committee is responsible for the most important part of the conference: the sessions and speeches. It is the role of this committee to find the most stimulating and dynamic speakers possible. Most of the program committee's expenditures are for the purpose of obtaining speakers and planning an interesting and well-designed program. Here are some illustrative program expenditures:

E 1   Program committee (13%)
    1.1   General sessions speakers (stipends)
    1.2   Computer-assisted program schedule search
    1.3   Special workshops and discussion groups
    1.4   Audiovisual equipment
    1.5   Concurrent session supplies: signs, ribbons, badges, and so forth
    1.6   Support: clerical, duplication, supplies, and materials, postage, post office box, and telephone

Operations and Arrangements. Expenditures for the operations and arrangements committee amount to about 34 percent of total expenses. Some of these expenditures are defrayed by the conference special event and meal function revenues. Marketing is expecially important in this area so that expenditures can be offset by attendance. It is recommended that the coordinator attempt to underwrite such activities as the all-conference social and other association receptions, luncheons, and meetings through publishers and business and industry. Here are some expenditures for this committee:

2   Operations and arrangements (34%)
    2.1   All-conference social
    2.2   Special dinner activities
    2.3   Side tours
    2.4   Exhibit space rental (including exchange tables)
    2.5   Special arrangements

2.6 Hotel costs

2.7 Registration and necessary equipment

2.8 Meals and hospitality functions (meal tickets)

2.9 Technicians

2.10 Luncheons

2.11 Hospitality room

2.12 First aid room

2.13 Signs, badges, stickers, ribbons, portfolios

2.14 Security guards

2.15 Support: clerical, supplies and materials, postage and shipping, and telephone

Publicity, Promotion, and Information Committee. A significant amount of the expenditures of the publicity, promotion, and information committee is spent on marketing the conference for the purpose of increasing the number of registrants, improving the association's image, and increasing the conference's visibility. Marketing is particularly vital to the conference, since registration brings in around 65 percent of conference revenues. An analysis of past conference final reports will help in projecting future expenditures. For example, attendance is generally higher when there are well-advertised special airline discount flights to and from the conference site. Conference sites adjacent to several states that are within 200 miles of the conference are likely to stimulate one-day registrations. Such geographic factors as these can be taken into account in planning and budget preparation. As a general guideline, sites that do not have extra added incentives and attractions for participants may require additional money for creative marketing and promotion. Here are some illustrative expenditures for the publicity, promotion, and information committee:

E3 Publicity, promotion, and information (41%)

3.1 Preconference publicity and promotion

3.2 Paid advertising

3.3 Conference program books

3.4 Media relations/press kits

3.5 Mailhouse service and postage

3.6 Daily newsletter

3.7 Photographer

3.8 Printing

3.9 Support: clerical, supplies and materials, duplication (including copier at conference), telephone, and postage

Executive Committee. Executive committee meetings are held to plan and lay the groundwork for a conference. Over a year and a half, as many as eighteen meetings are held to plan and approve a conference theme, logo, evaluation questions and design, budget, time schedule, promotional plan, call for papers, conference brochures, and the conference program book. Here are some of the possible expenditures for the executive committee:

E4   Executive committee (3%)
     4.1   Meeting expenses
     4.2   Stationery, stickers
     4.3   Fiscal and narrative reports
     4.4   Awards
     4.5   Volunteer coordination
     4.6   Support: clerical, supplies and materials, telephone, postage

Evaluation Committee. The purpose of evaluation activities is to collect information that is important to the association and to subsequent conference planning committees. Here are some of the important questions: How satisfied were participants with conference logistics, such as the date, the site, the facilities, the activities, and the cost? How applicable or relevant was the program content to participants? How did professional subgroups, such as public school educators, military educators, continuing professional educators, and community-based educators respond to the conference program? Evaluation expenses can include the following:

E5   Evaluation committee (1%)
     5.1   Computer forms
     5.2   Computer data reports
     5.3   Printing of evaluation reports
     5.4   Support: clerical, supplies and materials, telephone, postage

Staff Travel Expenses. The purpose of staff travel expenses is to provide paid staff or volunteers with funds for lodging, meals, and mileage or transportation based on a previously established schedule. These expenses may or may not be met by conference planners.

E6.   Staff travel expenses (6%)
     6.1   Lodging
     6.2   Subsistence
     6.3   Mileage or transportation

Contingency Expenses. The contingency expenses category is an emergency "profit margin" designed to meet unplanned and unexpected expenses.

E7   Contingency expenses (2%)
     7.1   Unplanned, unexpected expenses

Administration of Budget and Finance. The conference fiscal officer works closely with the general conference chairperson and other designated persons to establish a ledger and a fiscal system that includes requisition of payments, purchase orders, vendor invoicing, and a monthly reporting system. The next four paragraphs describe an informal but tried and proved system (Copeland, 1983).

Purchase Requisition System. The general conference chairperson or the coordinators submit purchase requisition forms to the fiscal officer, who rejects or approves each request. If a request is rejected, the fiscal officer marks it rejected and returns it to the appropriate requester. A request should be approved only when it lies within the budget allocation.

Purchase Orders. All the purchase requisitions should be numbered, and the fiscal officer and general conference chairperson must account for all purchase orders used and not used. Both the general chairperson and the fiscal officer have authority to access the purchase orders. Copies of approved purchase orders are signed, one copy is sent to the vendor, and another copy is filed by the fiscal officer with the conference records.

Vendor Invoicing. Vendors typically require an authorized purchase order to be able to render services or sell products for the conference. The vendor must enter the purchase order number on all invoices. Invoices submitted without purchase order numbers are returned to vendors. On receipt of a purchase order and rendering of a service or delivery of a product, the vendor can then invoice conference headquarters.

Reporting. It is recommended that the planners and the fiscal officer be furnished with a monthly report of expenditures and remaining balance of budget allocations.

An understanding of human behavior undergirds the effective team-building effort that is necessary in conducting successful conferences. The human side of conference planning is just as important as the ideas, the concepts, and the budget. The general chairperson needs to be well organized, to pay close attention to detail, and to possess leadership skills related to motivation, communication, delegation, problem solving, decision making, and conflict resolution. These skills can help to keep communication open, free flowing, and smooth. Leadership skills alone do not make a conference successful, but the lack of such skills can destroy a conference. The quality of large conferences depends on how well the program and budget are planned, how well the arrangements are executed, and how well the conference is publicized. However, in the final analysis, the quality of large conferences depends on how well all conference volunteers carry out their responsibilities.

References

Cope, J. L. "The Development of a Process for Planning the Evaluation Component of National Adult Education Conferences." Unpublished dissertation, University of Pittsburgh, 1981.

Cope, J. L. *National Adult Education Conference, 1983: Final Report.* Indiana, Penn.: Indiana University of Pennsylvania, 1984.

Cope, J. L., and Leahy, M. A. *National Adult Education Conference, 1983: Progress Report.* Indiana, Penn.: Indiana University of Pennsylvania, 1982.

Copeland, B. *1983 National Adult Education Conference: On-Site Procedures for Registration.* Washington, D.C.: American Association for Adult Continuing Education, 1983.

Maloney, C. *National Adult Education Conference, 1984: Final Report.* Louisville, Ky.: University of Louisville, 1985.

Robinson, R. *National Adult Education Conference, 1985: Progress Report.* W ashington, D.C.: American Association for Adult Continuing Education, 1985.

Smith, W., and others. *Closing Report, 1980.* St. Louis, Mo.: National Adult Education Conference, 1980.

Standing Service Unit on National Conference. *National Adult Education Conference: Procedures Manual.* Washington, D.C.: American Association for Adult and Continuing Education, 1983.

Judith L. Cope is assistant professor of adult education at Kent State University. She was the general chairperson of the 1983 National Adult Education Conference.

If Murphy's Law has applicability anywhere, it is in conference planning.

Problems and Setbacks, and Strategies for Avoiding Them

Sandra A. Ratcliff

The worst can happen at any stage in the planning of a conference. In fact some problems can be serious enough to warrant postponement of several or all of the activities. This chapter describes eight such problems and provides ideas for meeting each one before it becomes unmanageable. These are the addressed problems: shortage of sufficient lead time, resignation of a committee chair, duplication or misunderstanding of a committee member's duties, registration or budget problems, cancellation of the main speaker, illness or a job change for the conference chair, complaints at the conference, and problems with the hotel.

Shortage of Sufficient Lead Time

Chapter One describes a conference planning process. Let us assume that the conference planner is short on time. That is, there is not enough lead

The author wishes to express her appreciation to Dennis G. Carlstedt, director of sales and marketing at Lodge of the Four Seasons, Lake of the Ozarks, formerly of Pheasant Run Inn, St. Charles, Illinois, for help and advice provided during several conferences.

P. J. Ilsley (Ed.). *Improving Conference Design and Outcomes.* New Directions for Continuing Education, no. 28. San Francisco: Jossey-Bass, December 1985.

time to plan and organize the committee, budget, evaluation, and other activities properly. By taking strong and swift steps, a conference planner can still make the conference a success.

The first step is to organize thoroughly, an aspect of planning that is extremely critical when lead time is short. Second, before assembling a committee, the conference planner will benefit by brainstorming and making a list of every conference task to be accomplished. Each item on the list should then be written on a separate sheet of paper together with details involved in its accomplishment. Third, under each detail, the names of possible committees and chairs should be listed. Fourth, a target date should be noted for each task, even if it seems unrealistic at this point. Fifth, additional thoughts or ideas related to the accomplishment of any task should be written in as they occur. Five headings exemplify the process: Task to be accomplished, Details, Names of Committees-chairs, Dates to be completed, Comments.

A helpful tip for the conference planner is that he or she should walk away from the completed charts and lists for a period of time, then return to them for the purpose of making revisions. Often a break is needed to catch mistakes in planning that one passes over in the intensity of the moment. In addition, it is wise to bring in another person to react to the plans, details, and timelines. Besides helping to organize the conference, this process of mapping a strategy and its aspects on paper also helps to make the work seem manageable in the planner's own mind.

The next step is to delegate. The importance of delegating cannot be overemphasized, especially if lead time is short. Conference planning can take over the major part of planner's lives even when they have sufficient lead time. Under critical circumstances, all aspects of planning are intensified, because deadlines overlap, frustration mounts, and the quality of the conference may be in jeopardy. The best alternative is to find good, dependable conference committee chairs. Criteria for a chair should include the ability to make decisions on one's own, the willingness to abide by deadlines, access to communication resources (phones, secretarial help, copying machines) initiative and creativity, and finally, the time needed to do the work.

When committee chairs have been selected, a planning meeting should be held to assign the responsibilities. It is very important for each person to understand his or her duties. With each duty should come a realistic timeline. (The only thing more frustrating than missing a deadline is missing several deadlines.) This planning meeting should be thorough, with all duties spelled out, all timelines set, and names suggested for possible committee chairs. Immediately after the meeting, the conference chair should make a chart with names, duties, and timelines and distribute it to all committee chairs. This measure alone can prevent small problems from becoming big ones. Likewise, a conference chair must often don the mantle of authority to prevent problems with committee chairs.

When lead time is short, preconference publicity is difficult. After organizing the conference, delegating assignments, and setting timelines, the conference chair's next most important job is to promote the conference. When it comes to advertising, the general rule is the sooner, the better. Even if nothing but the dates, location, and theme has been decided, those pieces of information should be publicized in the press, newsletters, and journals, if possible a year in advance. Try to have the keynote speaker or a topic for the keynote speech and a schedule ready for the first brochure.

After the first brochure is out, the next task is to compile the topics and presenters for the rest of the program. The result should take the form of the final brochure, which, in order to be helpful to participants, should arrive at least one and a half months before the conference. Any presenter not confirmed by then should be listed as "to be determined" or "to be assigned" together with the title of the topic. The more detail the final brochure contains, the more useful it is in recruiting participants. Participants like to see a detailed brochure in order to make choices for daily attendance.

Lack of lead time is not automatically a disaster, nor does it require one to resign from one's job in order to manage conference operations. It does mean that the effort has to be especially well organized, that committee roles need be assigned to competent people, and that realistic timelines need be set and followed.

Resignation of a Committee Chair

Conference committee chairs sometimes announce that they are resigning. When they do, a prepared conference chair is ready to step in and make adjustments. The extent of the adjustments depends on when the chair drops out, who else is working on the committee, and how well-defined the tasks are. Sometimes it is more efficient for a conference chair to take over the committee than it is to appoint someone else.

The timing of the resignation of the committee chair can make all the difference. The most preferable time for a committee chair to drop out is right at the beginning. Of course, this seldom happens. Chairs usually wait to resign until they believe they can no longer manage, too late in the planning or, as Murphy's Law would have it, at the worst possible moment.

The first step is to act, rather than to wait for the chair to change his or her mind. A call requesting a meeting in the chair's office (to avoid the possible excuse of travel time) is the best action. Approach the committee chair matter-of-factly, without being condescending or critical. The only issue at stake is the task of continuing the conference planning. Acquire plans, job assignments, timelines, and notes. Avoid waiting for typed notes; take what ever is available. Once the materials have been sorted into four categories—work accomplished, work to be dome, timeline, and names of persons working on specific tasks—they will be of great value.

If one week after the chair's resignation it has still not been possible to meet or if plans have not been received, the conference planner should call a meeting of the persons who have been working on the chair's committee. Committee members should be asked to describe the work accomplished, the work yet to be done, the timeline, and to identify those who have been working on specific tasks. If the chair has resigned soon after taking the job, seek a volunteer from the committee to lead it. If the committee chair has resigned halfway through planning or later, the best solution may be to assume the responsibility rather than find someone else.

In the event that the committee chair is unavailable for a meeting, has not sent plans, and has not appointed committee members, the easiest solution is to find a new chair, help him or her get committee members together and have tasks, timelines, and details ready for them. Regardless of the timing of the resignation of the committee chair, the conference chair will need to be ready to step in. The key word is *act*. To wait for a committee chair to change his or her mind or to provide thorough, typed plans is not only a mistake—it can actually mean increased work and aggravation for the conference planner.

Duplication and Misunderstanding of Duties

The role of a conference planner can include refereeing and arbitration if (committee members') duties and roles are not explicit. The best way to prevent duplication and misunderstanding of duties is to conduct committee meetings.

Shortly after a meeting with chairs, a meeting with all committee members is helpful. At that time, charts, grids, and so forth with everyone's name on them and with all duties assigned should be handed out. Each committee's assignments should be covered one by one. Committee members should have time to ask questions or clarify misunderstandings. No one should leave the meeting with confusion or questions. Each person should be provided with an organizational chart that lists duties and names. For those not in attendance, letters and charts help keep communication flowing.

Of course, owing to varying levels of enthusiasm, duplication or misunderstanding of duties may occur regardless of the number of planning meetings. A conference planner can be so involved with a conference that committee members' enthusiasm or lack of enthusiasm can go unnoticed. An overenthusiastic committee member views the assignment as a lifetime opportunity. Not content to do just a satisfactory job, he or she is on the phone every day with late-breaking news. Such individuals often take on the duties of other persons. Moreover, they like to keep on the phone. A conference chair who has more than one overenthusiastic person can get as many as thirty phone calls per week. If a conference chair becomes inaccessible, the overeager committee member may then call other committee planners. It happens in virtually every conference, and it must be handled tactfully early in the planning stages. Otherwise, committee members can become angered and lose their enthusiasm. An unenthusiastic committee member will not create the same problem, but such a person may still anger other committee chairs. For this reason, it is important to check the progress, or the lack of progress, of all committee members throughout the planning process and take steps accordingly.

Once committee chairs have been appointed, they should receive authority, not merely responsibility, to make decisions and run their committees. It is tempting for a conference planner to believe that he or she should make every decision and handle every problem. That belief is not only impractical, it can lead to disaster. It simply is not feasible for a conference, especially a conference with more than a thousand participants, to be run by a single person. As a conference grows in size, the number of decisions to be made multiplies. When chairs or members complain they should be listened to. Sometimes all that is necessary is for the conference planner to become aware of a problem.

Registration and Budget Problems

Registration numbers are always uncertain. The best preventive measure for low registration is early advertising. One general rule for conference advertising is identical to the rule for conference planning: The earlier the better. If the brochures have been well prepared, if the presenters and program are worth listening to, and if the conference advertising has been done with sufficient lead time, attendance should be no problem. If every effort has been made to advertise and registration is still low, the solution may be to increase the financial incentives for registration. Special offers, contests, media coverage, linkage with other activities, and special events are all ways of encouraging registration.

One idea is to offer a break on the registration fee for the second person from the same institution. Another is to give three or more persons a special price. Penalties for late registration can be withdrawn. Still another idea is to post one-day registration fees. Raffles and drawings for registrants are sometimes popular. The prizes can include books, materials, or free registration to another conference. Perhaps goals can be reached by stepping up the promotional campaign. To do so, you can either hire a public relations person to provide ideas and make contacts, or you can have volunteers conduct phone campaigns, send special mailers to prospective participants, or issue well-timed press releases. By contacting the Chamber of Commerce or convention center at the conference site, you may find that special activities are occurring immediately before or after the conference date. Travel packages can then be provided. Finally, the conference committee can meet to brainstorm ideas for interesting and unusual activities that can be added to the agenda. These activities include films, book fairs, dances, golf tournaments, races, and meet-the-authors. All these activities can induce participation.

Suppose it is one week before the conference, you have tried all the suggestions just listed, and registration is still low. First, the conference planner needs to be sure of the audience. For many conference groups, it is traditional to wait and register just a few days in advance. If it appears certain that registration will be low, several options are still available to prevent losing a lot of money. All these options involve reducing conference expenses.

First of all, cut down the meal count. Arrangements should have been made with the hotel for a twenty-four- or forty-eight-hour notice on meal counts. Be conservative, because the hotel percentage for additional place settings is usually merely five to ten percent. A rule of thumb is to figure your number then reduce it by five percent. Second, cut out coffee breaks. Although most conference groups have been programmed to expect coffee at break time, they are able to find the coffee shop, and they rarely become upset if coffee is not provided. Coffee is expensive and a luxury that can be cut if need be. Third, if the hotel is charging for meeting rooms and programs have not been printed, presenters can double up in the same room. While this option may seem awkward, it is just as awkward for a presenter to address two or three people. Given the choice, a presenter might prefer a shorter session and more participants. If programs have been printed and the idea is agreeable, simply provide a correction sheet. Sessions can be lively if several presenters give their viewpoints and time is allowed for questions. Fourth, if presenters are being paid, special precautions must be taken. Perhaps they will lower the fee under certain circumstances or it may be necessary to cancel their engagement.

It is never pleasant to spend a lot of time and effort in planning a conference and then have attendance or budget problems. Applying a few austerity measures can help.

Cancellation of the Main Speaker

Cancellation of the main speaker at a conference can be a big disappointment. The conference planner will have to make a quick decision. There are several options.

First, you can cancel the conference. If the main speaker is the key to the entire conference, the best solution may indeed be to cancel rather than provide a less attractive conference. It would be a good idea to find a date for rescheduling before all the registrants are notified. It may take the edge off their disappointment.

Second, you may be able to get another speaker. If arrangements for the main speaker have been made through an aide or agent, ask that person for the names of substitutes. If the presenter is from public office, he or she may have an aide who knows the topic to be discussed equally well. If several persons have been approached to speak for the conference and only one has been chosen, ask one of them if he or she would like to step in. If advertising is already out and a second mailing is impossible, use a flyer to advertise the new speaker, and hand it out at the registration desk.

Third, you can have a debate or panel presentation instead. If the cancelled speaker was the only one with the knowledge (this seems very unlikely) or if a suitable replacement cannot be found, a lively debate or panel combined with questions and comments from the audience can be an effective substitute. Since keynote speakers rarely provide for audience participation, an audience-focused debate or panel may prove to be a nice change.

Fourth, you can simply eliminate the keynote address. A conference can go on without one. If one purpose of a keynote address is to get all the participants together at one time, the time set aside for it could be spent brainstorming issues or problems, discussing concerns, outlining the conference, and announcing housekeeping details or providing entertainment instead.

Cancellation of the main speaker is unlikely and usually unexpected, but, like every other problem mentioned in this chapter, it can be worked around with a little creativity and forethought.

Illness or Job Change of the Conference Chair

Regardless of the size of a conference or the significance of the event, life goes on, meaning that events happen. One of the most difficult problems to handle is illness or a job change for the conference chair during conference planning. Plans can be adjusted according to the current stage of planning.

In the early stages of conference planning, when the operation has been in effect for only a short period of time and committee members have hardly worked together, it may be best for a chair to step down or to act in another, less responsible role. The first planning stages are the busiest and most complicated; thus they are the most difficult. If work is neglected during the early planning stage, a conference cannot run smoothly. A very clear assessment of problems that illness or a job change brings should be made. Conference planning should be the first and foremost consideration. Another opportunity to run a conference may come again.

In the middle of conference planning, it is more difficult to get a new chair. A conference chair should have knowledge about the conference that no one else has. Again, depending on the seriousness of the illness or the pressures of the new job, the conference chair may need to take a break for several weeks and then resume responsibility. Such a move may necessitate the appointment of a temporary chair, accompanied by a detailed orientation. Another alternative is to have a committee chair take over communications for several weeks until the chair can take the lead again. Either way, pressing a permanent cochair into service or finding a temporary chair will mean that the conference continues as planned.

Naturally, it is a problem if the conference planner becomes ill or takes a new job; this development is most manageable in the final stages of the planning process. If planning is thorough, the conference rolls on with or without a conference planner. In such an event, it would be worthwhile for one committee chair to call the others together for an update and to divide up the reponsibilities for work that remains to be completed. Again, depending on the seriousness of the illness, or the nature of the new job, the conference planner may still be able to share concerns, assignments, or issues.

The timing and seriousness of illness and new job assignments will dictate in part the action to be taken to replace or help the conference chair. The stage of conference planning will further affect the decisions that need to be made. Regardless of these factors, the conference will still go on.

Complaints at the Conference

Nothing is more unnerving than to spend six months to a year or more of one's life planning a conference and still get complaints. Nevertheless, it is inevitable. Complaints are lodged at all parts of conferences. Handling them without getting discouraged is the key.

Keeping on schedule, often presents problems. Planning a realistic schedule is the best way of preventing such problems. The bigger the group, the more time is needed for movement to and from sessions. Luncheon speakers should be given time frames and reminded of the time five minutes before they are due to finish. Sessions should start and end on time; it makes a big difference to presenters and participants alike. If the conference chair stays on schedule, the whole conference seems to run a little smoother.

Complaints about the hotel are frequent. First, a conference planner should realize that people complain about service regardless of its quality. We become accustomed to our own schedules, our comforts at home, which means that a hotel may never satisfy everyone. When complaints occur about such things as air-conditioning, heating, food, bugs or other pests, the cleanliness of rooms, or service, steps should be taken to resolve them. Once the proceedings have gotten under way, there may not be enough time for effective recourse. Certainly, flagrant violations of the contract and guests, criticisms should be communicated in writing to hotel management as well to corporate headquarters if the hotel belongs to a franchise. Comments can sometimes be heard years later; for example, "Remember the conference when we had soggy potato chips?" "Remember the year when the boiler went out and we had cold showers?" or "Remember the runny eggs and the salad that had a worm in it?" Unfortunately, an otherwise great conference may be remembered as the one with the soggy potato chips or the runny eggs.

Complaining, nervous committee members can present a problem. Committee chairs and members may be more nervous and concerned about their part than a conference chair who has responsibility for the entire undertaking. By providing time for dialogue with committees throughout the conference, a conference planner may be able to defuse such anxiety and help to resolve the issues. By meeting with committee members the evening before or by hosting a private hospiality for committee members only, the planner can give them an opportunity to vent their concerns and to see their efforts for what they are—part of the whole. A breakfast meeting seems also to be a good time to defuse anxieties.

A problem table is one very effective way of dealing with problems before they get out of hand. Posting a troubleshooter at the registration desk may be all that is required to handle most problems. Such a person can be particularly invaluable for handling minor problems.

Registration seldom operates without complaints or problems. It is one of the most problem-laden aspects of a conference. A thorough orientation for registration volunteers can prevent inappropriate behavior on their part when they must deal with conflict. The attitude of registration volunteers sets the tone of a conference; training them is well worth the time and effort. It is best to have a sufficient number of registration volunteers so that, through rotation, they can all enjoy and participate in some of the conference activities.

Complaints are to be expected. The ease with which they are handled can make a conference a positive experience for everyone involved.

Problems with Hotels

Problems with a hotel can be major or minor. Establishing a good working relationship with the hotel sales department and planning with its staff are both invaluable. However, even with thorough planning and good rapport with the sales department, a variety of problems can be anticipated. The discussion that follows highlights several common problems and ways of dealing with them quickly and efficiently.

It sometimes happens that room rates increase shortly before the conference is due to begin. Prevention is the best solution to this problem. When you book a conference, you can have single and double room rates written into the conference contract. This contract is binding, and the rates cannot legally be raised. Discuss rates in the negotiations, especially when you are booking a year or more in advance. If the best that sales staff can offer is a verbal agreement, discuss the possibility of the rates' being raised, and find out when the raise is anticipated. Although a hotel may not want to have the rates written into the contract one or two years in advance, that is only legal way for conference planners to ensure that rates will remain the same. It is wise to check with the sales department before brochures are printed.

Registrants become rightfully angry at unexpected increases in rates, and they may not attend because of it.

Some hotels charge for services at union rates. Ask the hotel if it is a union hotel. If it is, find out which unions it has, and plan accordingly. If the hotel has unions, extra expenses can be anticipated in several areas: Union hotels charge as much as $75 per box for materials carried from cars to rooms. Some unions are very strict and do not allow book salespersons or bands, for example, to carry their own boxes and equipment. Clear this with management before the conference. Hookups for displays using electrical outlets often have to be done by an electrician for a fee. Regardless of whose electrical cord it is or who plugs it in, the fee is charged. Once again, determine the policy beforehand. And never assume that electrical outlets or extension cords will be available; always ask first. Union hotels may not permit nonunion musical groups to entertain. If a disk jockey or band is selected, clear it with the hotel first. Also, electricians and stagehands will have to be hired to assist with live performances. The rates should be determined beforehand. Finally, cash bars require hotel bartenders, and the fee schedule is based on the number of drinks sold. Owing to the fact that per hour charges and the cost of liquor can vary considerably, getting a written agreement is an important method of price protection.

The serving of food is the third major area of problems related to hotels. Whenever food is served, even if it is only coffee, a gratuity is often automatically charged (currently 16 to 20 percent). Determine the amount of the gratuity, and plan accordingly. While negotiation here is possible, it is unlikely to be successful. Groups with tax-exempt status can ease the burden somewhat by presenting a tax identification number.

Take care that the meal count is accurate, and consider the types of food to be served. The size of the group automatically causes some restrictions. Soup is not recommended for groups exceeding fifty (it is too difficult to keep hot). Buffets work well, but be sure that hotel staff or the conference planner directs the participants to speed up the process. A single line for 300 or more persons adds hours to the meal time.

To be frank, while soup gets cold, ice cream melts. Avoid both. Avoid fish—complaints are inevitable. Chicken is very popular, but it may be too commonplace for some. Salads may suffice for the entree, but hearty eaters often complain when meat is not served. Last, provide for vegetarians (generally 5 percent of the group) by asking the kitchen have vegetable plates ready. The caterer may be able to provide creative suggestions that can make the meals attractive; conference planners should keep an open mind.

Hospitalities and receptions are an important part of most conferences, and, as veteran conference planners know, they require planning. Hotels commonly have policies regarding hospitality suites. For low-budget conferences, a hospitality room may need to be set up with liquor and supplies purchased outside the hotel. To reduce expenses even more, each participant can help to defraying costs by purchasing drinks. Two problems can occur with this austerity measure: The hotel may charge a corkage fee, and some participants may fail to donate the money. The hotel policy on hospitality will determine your options. At the best, the hotel will have an out of sight, out of mind policy that eliminates the possible fees. At the same time, it can be a mistake to have a hospitality without notifying management. Parties tend to become noisy, and charges for the room can be expensive. If the hotel does not allow the conference committee to provide its own liquor and supplies, there will be a corkage fee, bartender's fee, and room rent. This can become expensive. If expenses are to be recouped on a per drink or one-time volunteer basis, it is a good idea to determine a price, sell tickets or hospitality stickers for badges at the registration desk, and monitor entrance to the site. Neither tickets nor badges are foolproof, but either one is much better than having a pot for contributions.

Problems with parking and public transportation can mar a conference. Negotiations with the hotel should include determination of parking privileges. The hotel should also provide information about access to airports, train stations, and bus lines and roads and highways leading to the hotel. Perhaps even more important is the planner's assessment of the security within the area. If safety in the area is a concern, an escort service should be provided. To prevent complaints from conference registrants, the conference planner should ask questions regarding a hotel's policies on reservations and on check-in and check-out times. The following questions will help to clarify potential problems: What is the cutoff date for hotel reservations? Three weeks, two weeks, or less? Do rates increase after the cutoff date? Is there a weekend package if participants want to arrive before or stay after the conference date? What is the check-in time? What is the check-out time? What credit cards does the hotel accept? Are deposits required? Do meeting room costs increase if the number of overnight rooms booked falls below expectations? Once again, keeping an eye on reservation numbers, costs, and problems can prevent major problems for participants.

Coffee breaks are crucial in pacing a conference and in providing the informality needed to promote social exchange among conference participants. Two concerns raised by coffee breaks are timing and convenience. The timing of coffee breaks is actually of little concern unless the hotel is late in serving. It is a good idea to check one half hour or at least fifteen minutes ahead of the break to make sure that everything has been set up. The other potential problem with coffee breaks involves location. If there are only several meeting rooms, the coffee can be placed in the back of each room. For large conferences, it may be best to have two or three different sites for coffee. All sites should be directly outside the meeting room or in a hallway close by.

The last potential problem with hotels involves meeting-room arrangements. Meeting-room setups should be discussed in advance. The following questions are intended to facilitate discussion: What meeting rooms will be used? Are they close together? Are maps needed? If rooms are on various levels, how long will it take participants to move from one area to the next? How many elevators are available? Does the hotel provide for the handicapped? How many can be seated in a room? Consider three arrangements: conference style, theater style, and circles. Are extra chairs readily available? Who is to be called for help with equipment in meeting rooms? Are podiums, screens, and microphones available? Are there electric outlets in all rooms?

One good rule to follow in preconference negotiations with hotel management is to ask about its future plans for renovation. If renovation is imminent and you have to use the hotel, realize that renovation often takes longer than anticipated, and plan accordingly.

Cancellation of a hotel contract may mean the end of a conference. If a hotel cancels, ask its help in procuring another hotel. Check back with the other hotels that bid for the conference. Make sure that all contracts signed by hotel management are legally binding.

Conclusion

Altogether, planning and conducting a conference is a great thrill that brings about a real sense of accomplishment. Problems are to be expected, but they do not have to be greater than the rewards of the conference planning itself. All the problems described in this chapter have actually happened to me during the past five years. Anticipating such problems is the biggest asset in handling them. Conferences can be fun! Just be prepared.

Sandra A. Ratcliff is assistant director for instructional services at the Illinois Institute for Continuing Legal Education.

*Planners, presenters, and participants must be aware of
environmental factors that affect their experience if a conference
is to be successful.*

Creating an Optimal Conference Environment

Reginald Foucar-Szocki

This chapter addresses the environmental factors of space, temperature, lighting, color, and the human element and their relationship to conferencing. Practical ideas for conference planners and participants follow the discussion of each factor.

Space

Spatial relationships, interior decorating, and the physical layout of a room make a difference on the perception and performance of the people within it. The importance of a room that is esthetically pleasing for all the senses cannot be emphasized enough. The conference planner can increase the probability of participant success at conferences by being aware of physical space. Canter (1968) found that four elements are associated with esthetics: friendliness, coherence, comfort, and pleasantness. Participants are less likely to give assistance in rooms that are cluttered, rooms with sizes and shapes that conflict, rooms that contain a multiplicity of various objects, and rooms that are poorly set up. (Sherrod and others, 1977; Lambert, 1981).

The author wishes to thank Mr. Norbert Henry, program administrator of University College, Syracuse University, for assistance in preparing this chapter.

P. J. Ilsley (Ed.). *Improving Conference Design and Outcomes.* New Directions
for Continuing Education, no. 28. San Francisco: Jossey-Bass, December 1985.

For these reasons, presenters should check out the site in advance if at all possible. They should look at the styles and types of chairs in the room and the image that the room presents. They should see how their voice carries in the room. If they plan to use overheads or slides, they should be sure that everyone in attendance can see what they are projecting. They should find out whom to call if the audio visual equipment fails. If the presenter finds that a session for thirty has been scheduled for a room that holds two hundred, he or she should rearrange the room immediately to create an environment that is appropriate for the actual number of participants.

Temperature

A comfortable temperature is necessary for successful conferencing; there is a relationship between attentiveness, awareness, productivity, and temperature. Creating a comfortable learning environment is difficult without maintenance of proper temperature control.

The effect of temperature on performance has been well researched over the past sixty years. Vernon and Beford (1929) found that men loading coal slowed progressively as the temperature reached 62 degrees Fahrenheit. As the temperature increased beyond 76 degrees, frequent rest breaks became necessary. Studies of Morse code operators (Macworth, 1946) showed an acceptable range of mistakes when the temperature was between 80 and 92 degrees. However, mistakes quadrupled, when the temperature rose to 100 degrees. Finally, a study of weight lifting (Eckenrode and Abbot, 1953) found that six times as much weight could be lifted at 60 degrees as when the temperature was 110 degrees. All these studies underline that performance decreases as temperature increases. Extreme cold has not been researched as highly, but common sense suggests that extremes of cold affect performance. The optimum temperature can vary with task, age, sex, weight, amount of clothing worn, and location.

There is no one optimum temperature for effective performance. Studies have shown that people over 40 prefer slightly higher temperatures than people under 40. Likewise, a person doing physical work may be comfortable in a cool environment, whereas someone doing sedentary work in the same environment will feel cold. Someone dressed heavily will be uncomfortable in a room temperature set at 75 or 80 degrees, whereas someone dressed lightly may be content (Kazarian, 1984). Temperature is a critical environmental factor in successful conferencing. The point is that extremes at either end of the scale can create negative learning environment.

For these reasons, rooms equipped with individually controlled, accessible thermostats are preferable. Conference planners should make sure that participants in the back of the room can hear the presenter even when the air conditioning or heating fan is on. Planners should ask presenters to consider the following statements: Be aware of participants' needs in regard to temperature. Will they be too hot or too cold? Find out how to control heat, ventilation, and air conditioning within the room. If it cannot be controlled from within, find out whom in the hotel to phone. If you are an active presenter, realize that you will be expending more energy than participants: You may be warm, but they may not be. Dress accordingly. Ventilation can be promoted by opening a window or keeping the door open.

Participants should find out the temperature and climate of the conference city at the time scheduled for the conference. Participants should take jacket, sweater, or coat to a session if they are at all unsure. Participants should look for the heat or air conditioning vents in the room and take their seats accordingly. Being comfortable in a conference room increases awareness, retention, and enjoyment.

Lighting

The lighting in a conference room is another important environmental factor to consider. For example, insufficient lighting can quickly lead to eyestrain and fatigue. In presentations that require participants to study minute details, such a crowded overhead transparencies, participants need relatively high levels of illumination. Presentations using lecture or small-group formats also need relatively high levels of illumination. Research demonstrates that proper illumination increases work output by 10 to 20 percent. (Kazarian, 1984). An effective lighting system provides uniform illumination over the entire surface area without shadows or glare. Rooms with numerous low-wattage bulbs are more effective than rooms with a few high-wattage bulbs.

Glare is direct or indirect. Direct glare results when the light source falls directly into an observer's eyes, as when one looks directly into the sun. Indirect glare comes from a reflection of light into the observer's eyes, as when a driver picks up the high beams of the car behind him in his rearview mirror.

The *Lighting Handbook* of the Illuminating Engineering Society (1972) has a complete listing of recommended footcandle levels for every room, ranging from a lecture room (70 footcandles) to a classroom with a chalkboard (150 footcandles).

Planners should look at the type and source of lights when considering the conference rooms. They should determine whether lights are on dimmers and whether one set of lights can be off while the others are on. They should consider how the room will handle overheads, films, and slides. There are several ways of overcoming direct glare: by reducing the brightness of the light source, by using low- instead of high-wattage bulbs, and by increasing the brightness surrounding the glare source itself; this has the same effect as reducing the glare. There are several ways of overcoming indirect glare: by using diffused or indirect lighting, by providing a good level of illumination around the reflecting surface, and by selecting the appropriate surface material painted versus wallpapered rooms).

Participants should select a seat directly under the lights if the presentation requires extensive reading or writing during the session. Sitting near a window is another way of being sure that one has additional natural light; however, the participant should realize that there is a potential for glare.

Color

Color is a factor in the development of mood and atmosphere because it has an effect on our emotions and feelings. An all-day presentation in a room painted fire engine red will be a challenge. General knowledge of color allows a presenter to combat potential negative factors. The idea is to overcome the feelings created by inappropriate room color.

Goldstein (1942) and Kazarian (1984) associated color with specific feelings, emotions, and sensations. The following list summarizes their findings.

Red: Excitement, violence, aggression, stimulation of activity
Blue: Cooling effect, relaxation, and easy on the eyes
Gray: Cold and depressing
Green: Operates contrary to red, sedates and quiets
Yellow: Cheery, stimulating and attention-drawing
White: Spaciousness
Black: Heaviness and smallness

Kazarian (1984) states that a person exposed to predominantly red colors may exhibit increased blood pressure, quickened muscular reactions, and heightened emotions. In contrast, persons exposed mainly to blues and greens tend to exhibit slower muscular response and quicker mental and conversational responses.

Lack of contrast caused by the predominance of a single color makes it difficult for a person to distinguish objects. Even the color green, restful and sedate as it is, will lead to eye and body fatigue if it is used on its own. In a small room light colors give the illusion of space, while dark colors make the room appear even smaller. Warm colors should be used in windowless rooms to give a sense of space. Also, rooms that are highly reflective or that have too many colors in them can cause discomfort (Digerness, 1982).

For these reasons, planners should check all presentation rooms and record their size, color, and seating capacity. Moreover, planners should be aware that the color of a room can have an effect on the presenters as well as on their audience. Planners who are forced to use presentation rooms of different colors should schedule presenters based on the color of the room and their presentation style. A presenter who includes movement and action should be in a blue or a green room. A presenter who will be giving a lecture should not. Planners should let presenters know well in advance that they are going to work in a windowless room that has a horrible color. Perhaps this will help them to prepare. In fact, planners should share general information about colors and association with presenters. Finally, presenters should understand that rearranging the room can mitigate the effects of color. For example, they can face the wall with the door, use small groups, face a wall with a contrasting color, ask for input from their audience, and use posters or flip charts to break up the color scheme.

Participants should be aware that the color of the room can have an effect on their readiness to participate in the session. They should use their knowledge of the effects of color to their advantage when attending sessions. Participants should let the presenter know about their difficulties with the color of the room, particularly if it affects their decision to stay or leave. The presenter will appreciate such information. To lessen the intensity of a room, participants can select a seat in the back third, this gives them a wider-angle view. Participants can also use relaxing exercises—closing their eyes, rolling their head—to give their body a break from the impact of the colors, contrast, or reflections.

The Human Element

The environmental factors just discussed are concrete. The final environmental factor to be considered is abstract and intangible. this factor falls under the umbrella heading of the human element. The human element is ongoing; it is the sense of belonging and of feeling that one is part of the group. The importance of this factor has been demonstrated by the use of quality circles in the workplace and more recently by the writings of Naisbitt (1982) and Peters and Waterman (1982).

It is the role of a presenter to set the climate or the mood in the session. This mood should give each participant the opportunity to gain from attending the session. Draves (1984) identifies numerous hands-on techniques aimed at increasing participant involvement and belonging. Smith (1982) introduces a learning how to learn concept that centers on the needs of the learner, individual learning styles, and training as an activity organized to increase learning.

Presenters need to be aware of the needs of adult learners and ways of maximizing their time together. Presenters should be responsible for understanding the importance of climate and appreciate their role in establishing it. If at all possible, presenters should check in the day before their presentation.

Participants should be willing to take risks in meeting other participants. They should identify clear expectations and goals for the conference. They should let the conference committee know their needs and wants; they should not be afraid or ashamed to state them to the proper person. Finally, the conference planner should make every effort to keep all participants and presenters informed, to have signs welcoming them at the airport, to provide a listing of alternatives for meals, and to respect the need of both participants and presenters for quiet or downtime.

In summary, one of the building blocks for a successful conference is facilities that are environmentally pleasing. The conference committee must go beyond the obvious actions of selecting a city, presenters, and scheduling sessions toward providing the additional accommodation that leads directly to a satisfactory conference experience. For example, the committee can consider that outstanding facilities provide large, colorful, well-ventilated, safe, and esthetically appealing rooms that allow for groupings of various sizes; these facilities also offer a variety of quality service options. If planners consider such issues, the chances for a successful conference are increased. Without environmentally pleasing facilities, even the most dynamic presentations may seem ordinary.

Both presenters and participants have an additional responsibility. A presenter has to be aware of the expectations and needs of the audience. The participant has to have a commitment to exploration, an ability to synthesize and adapt what is being presented, and a willingness to take responsibility for having his or her needs met. The idea is to provide an environment that is most conducive to this quest. The participant must have a sense of comfort, belonging, and safety. Once these needs have been met, the participant will be able to realize the full benefits of his or her conference experience.

References

Canter, D. "Office Size: An Example of Psychological Research in Architecture." *Architects Journal,* 1968, *147,* 881–888.

Digerness, B. "Color It Productive." *Administrative Management,* December 1982, pp. 46–50.

Draves, W. A. *How to Teach Adults.* Manhattan, Kans.: Learning Education Resources Network, 1984.

Eckenrode, R. T., and Abbot, W. C. *The Response to Man and His Environment.* Stanford, Conn.: Dunlap, 1959.

Goldstein, K. "Some Experimental Observations Concerning the Influence of Color on the Function of Organism."*Occupational Therapy and Rehabilitation,* 1942, *21,* 147–151.

Illuminating Engineering Society. *Lighting Handbook.* (5th ed.) New York: Illuminating Engineering Society, 1972.

Kazarian, E. A. *Work Analysis and Design for Hotels, Restaurants, and Institutions.* Westport, Conn.: AVI, 1984.

Kidd, J. R. *How Adults Learn.* New York: Cambridge, 1973.

Lambert, C. J. "Environmental Design: The Food Service Manager's Role." *The Cornell Hotel and Restaurant Administration Quarterly,* 1981, *22,* 62–68.

Macworth, N. H. "Effect of Heat on Wireless Telegraph Operators Hearing and

Recording Morse Messages." *British Journal of Independent Medicine,* 1946, *3,* 143–158.

Naisbitt, J. *Megatrends: Ten New Directions Transforming Our Lives.* New York: Warner Books, 1982.

Peters T., and Waterman, T. *In Search of Excellence: Lessons from America's Best-Run Companies.* New York: Harper & Row, 1982.

Sherrod, D. R., Armstrong, D., Hewitt, J., Madonia, B., Speno, S., and Teryua, D. "Environmental Attention, Affect, and Altruism." *Journal of Applied Social Psychology,* 1977, *4,* 359–371.

Smith, R. M. *Learning How to Learn.* New York: Cambridge, 1982.

Vernon, H. M., and Bedford, T. *The Relations of Atmospheric Conditions to the Working Capacity and the Accident Rate of Coal Miners.* IFRB Report No. 39. London: His Majesty's Stationery Office, 1927.

Reginald Foucar-Szocki is assistant professor of food management at Syracuse University. Previously he was assistant professor of food management at Buffalo State University College.

Participants learn to maximize the benefits of a conference
through strategizing and remaining open to the unanticipated.

How to Profit from Attending a Conference

Marcie Boucouvalas

Conferences are proliferating worldwide in a variety of forms and for a myriad of reasons. Despite the range in themes and types—international, national, regional, or local; general or special; open or invitational—all conferences face a cardinal challenge: Will participants choose to be conference consumers, or will they remain mere conference attenders?

Consuming by definition implies using up or exhausting the opportunity presented. A consumer is proactive in determining what he or she can derive from a conference. A consumer becomes a part of what is taking place. In contrast, *attending* denotes merely being present at; it implies a spectator role whereby one goes to sessions and even becomes involved in some activities but only reacts positively or negatively to what is offered and available. The proactive stance of the conference consumer—in attitude as well as in action—is missing from many conferences.

This chapter, addressed to conference goers as well as to conference planners, centers on the theme of conference consumption. The theme can be useful to both: Conference attenders can learn how to become conference consumers (even those who already consume conferences may find their horizons expanding), and planners can learn how to design a conference for consumption. The discussion that follows is based primarily on my own

P. J. Ilsley (Ed.). *Improving Conference Design and Outcomes.* New Directions
for Continuing Education, no. 28. San Francisco: Jossey-Bass, December 1985.

experience: discussions with conference planners and conference goers at a wide range of conferences over a number of years.

The chapter begins by exploring the meaning of conference consumption: the process involved in deciding to attend, the dynamics entailed in participating as a consumer in both attitude and action, and the transfer of learning after the conference is over. Next, it examines the functions that a conference can perform. Increased knowledge of what is possible can cultivate a consumer stance. In treating a conference as a meaningful learning experience, I will urge the reader to create an agenda that takes growth, expectations, and needs into account. Likewise, I will urge planning committees to design conferences so as to maximize consuming efforts. The discussion in this section complements the emphasis on the individual participant consumer and the conference as a personal experience by introducing the notion of learning community. The central section of this chapter describes a variety of nuts-and-bolts strategies for successful conference consumption. The chapter concludes by examining the notion of conference-consuming competencies and the relevance of theoretical, conceptual, and experimental information to the development of a conference-consuming competency model. This last section offers challenges to practitioners and researchers in regard to training and education for conference-consumption as well as needed research in the area. Since the notion of conference consumption is still in its infancy, I hope that the views conveyed in this chapter will challenge the reader to explore and contribute to this evolving area of inquiry.

Conference Consuming: Attitude Plus Action

Behaving and thinking as a conference consumer begins with the decision to attend. It proceeds through to the manner in which one participates in the conference, and it concludes with a personal evaluation of the conference as a learning experience, including what one has learned about being a better conference consumer. Conferences provide an opportunity not only to learn content but also to learn how to become a better learner.

Research indicates that marketing and promotional strategies have an effect on one's decision to participate in a conference. A conference consumer would be wise to understand such draws and consider the degree to which they affect one's decision. Becoming aware of how and why a person makes a choice to participate is an important first step in becoming a conference consumer both in attitude and in action.

The Conference as a Total Learning Experience

Once the decision to attend has been made, preplanning and strategizing, combined with an understanding of the plethora of incidental unplanned learning possibilities, are helpful in preparing participants to take a consumer stance. In this sense, it is important to consider the totality of a conference as a learning experience. For this reason, conference goers can profit from setting agendas before the conference and from reflecting on their expectations after the conference.

As Knowles (1980, p. 137) has noted, it is extremely important for us to "understand the various educational purposes a conference can serve," particularly since "the full potential of conferences . . . as formats for learning is far from being realized." Nadler and Nadler (1977, p. 2) add, "there is no end to the list of purposes for conferences because there will always be someone who will add, 'But I also use the conference for _____ .' "

These authors suggest that a number of educational purposes or learning experiences are common to conferences: information and materials, including facts presented; experiences shared; knowledge and skill acquired; problem solving, including the generating of new ideas and proposals and new ways of looking at old concerns; and the resulting bonus of commitment to action. The conference itself has an inspirational value, and the stimulation received from interaction with others *en masse* that often leads to new ideas and improved practice is important. The resulting improved attitude and psychological well-being that helps us in tackling challenges back home are equally important.

A seasoned conference consumer can creatively construct a professional conference agenda that often goes beyond the conference's stated purposes. For example, it is not at all uncommon to find participants attempting to hire or to be hired for consultancies or full-time jobs. Investigating graduate school possibilities is another part of some participants' agendas. Graduate student breakfasts provide opportunities for these participants. Finally, seeing old friends, renewing acquaintances, and developing new contacts—both personal and professional—have long been a tacit function of most conferences.

The Conference as a Learning Community

To develop strategies for successful conference consumption, it is useful for participants to understand the social patterns and learning communities. By virtue of their past involvement in a professional associa-tion, cohesion may already exist among many participants. An under-standing of the resulting social and professional dynamics can be useful for the conference consumer who wishes to participate fully.

If one is not familiar with the professional association or group that is hosting the conference, it is helpful to find out as much as possible about the sponsor as one can before one leaves for the conference. In fact, such information can help one to decide whether to attend. It is usually possible to obtain copy of the group's aims, scope, and objectives statement as well as a copy of its annual report from the group's headquarters. Information about the group's structure, including committees, interest groups, and chairs, can also be of use at the conference. However, information about these things is incomplete without an awareness of the people involved. Observing and continually asking questions may take courage, but it is a beneficial process. Subgroups form and stay together often for reasons beyond the guidelines on paper. Of course, the type of participant whom the conference attracts (for example, practitioners, researchers, or other groups) is an important piece of information that can sometimes be gleaned from information about previous conferences or from the preregistration list. When in doubt, ask.

In addition to the network of relationships and norms that already exists among many participants, important social dynamics and patterns evolve at conferences that can make it relatively easy or difficult to meet new people, make contacts, and create support structures. For example, the size, scope, geographical location, conference facilities, and conference format are all factors that influence a person's propensity to meet others. The dynamics will be different at conferences where participants eat together by design and at conferences in large cities where participants can rather easily disperse—sometimes for hours. A conference format based on a track design tends to propagate self-forming groups with similar interests.

So much incidental learning goes on at a conference that an attitude of openness and flexibility to opportunities seems imperative. Although it is difficult to generalize, it seems that the best time to meet many people is at the beginning of the conference (both at sessions and socials and at random) when a majority of participants have yet to find their security subgroups—a phenomenon that tends to occur as the conference progresses. Coming to the conference refreshed with a good night's sleep is a helpful precursor.

Strategies for Successful Conference Consumption

Equipped with knowledge of the vast range of possibilities available for consumption and learning at a conference and an appreciation that social dynamics already exist but that they can also be created, the conference participant is in a better position to construct and continually reconstruct strategies aimed at successful conference consumption. Whether the conference that one attends is local, state, regional, national, or international, open or invitational, there are general strategies that apply equally to the consumption of all conferences. However, one major difference can be in the expectations held—both by oneself and by others. For instance, the participants in an invitational conference are invited for a reason. A wise consumer in this situation would do well to learn exactly what expectations the conference planners have in mind. Of course, the responsibilities of the conference consumer differ if one is being sent by an employer. In this case, the participant may want to talk with his or her supervisor before leaving for the conference in order to clearly understand the supervisor's expectations. Conference consumption strategies may need to be adjusted in order to take the organizational development efforts of concern to one's employer into account.

When a conference reaches the proportion of national and international dimensions and when it is multidisciplinary in nature, the possibilities for consumption increase, but so do the potential barriers and frustrations. Sheer size and scope can be a bonus or a block.

Once one has made the decision to participate in a conference, one can start strategizing. Use of a conference planning sheet, a sample of which is provided in Figure 1, can be extremely beneficial, particularly if it is used as a preplanning tool. For example, some veteran conference goers write well in advance of the conference to specific presenters—even to a keynote speaker—whom they would like to meet expressing their interest in talking with them at the conference. This procedure is best followed up with a telephone call both to establish personal contact and to arrange a meeting time. If one is seeking information or opinion from a keynoter, it is best to be as specific as possible beforehand in order to make the best use of the limited time. Conference veterans find success in arranging a meal (or drink) with presenters. Breakfast is an especially good time, particularly since some people like to keep their day open for impromptu meetings and activities.

When it is not possible to prearrange contacts, one can approach an individual at the conference. One participant learned at the last minute that a speaker for the state conference had expertise in a specific research methodology in which she was interested. As soon as time and occasion permitted (which happened to be right after the speaker delivered the keynote address) she waited patiently, approached him, and said, "You're the main reason I've come to this conference. You have so much expertise, both theoretical and experiential, in a research method I'm interested in using. I'm well read about it and would like to share my project with you and learn more from you. When can we get together?"

Some first-time conference goers and students find these procedures a bit intimidating, particularly since not all presenters or big names have time (some may not have the energy or the interest) to meet at a conference in this manner. Often, they withdraw after an initial rebuff or what they interpret as such from a busy person.

Of course, even if none of the approaches just outlined works, the contact has still been made. As one long-time conference goer explained, "First, it's important not to take it personally. Look, you've made the contact, so you can always ask when, where and how you can reconnect with this individual at a later date. Then ask the person to recommend another human resource with whom you could talk in the interim."

A similar preplanning procedure can be used in many other areas on one's conference planning sheet. Attempting to build in as much success as

Figure 1. Sample Conference Planning Sheet

This outline can be used as a framework for preplanning one's conference agenda. Room should be left for further organizing goals and mapping out action steps as they arise at the conference. Activities can be elaborated or modified according to the needs of the individual. Keeping a specific log of daily activities and accomplishments as well as plans for use or follow-up after the conference are recommended.

ACTIVITY   *RESOURCES, CONTACTS, STRATEGIES*

Information and materials I am looking for:

Specific questions I want answered:

Problems I am trying to solve:

Things I want to learn or understand better:
    Knowledge
    Skill
    Attitude/value

People I want to meet (and why):
    Specific names:
     1.
      .
      .
    10.

    Types (representatives of positions,
      agencies, and so forth):

    Individuals from various contexts
      (government, business, industry,
      voluntary agencies, universities,
      community colleges, other):

    Individuals in specific positions
      (learning specialists, program
      directors, program developers,
      program evaluators, consultants,
      deans, faculty members, other):

Other Activities.

    Offered in conference design (for
      example, exhibits, socials)

    Created by self (for example, rump
      sessions, field trips)

Source: Revised from Boucouvalas and Brysh-Cooke (1982, p. 10).

possible before the conference begins is generally helpful. For example, one can contact the association or group that is hosting the conference to prearrange resources and contacts, both material and human. A computer list of conference preregistrants, which many hosts provide, can help in pinpointing resources and making contacts to achieve preestablished goals. Of course, these goals may have to be modified or elaborated on at the conference, and many serendipitous accomplishmemts may ensue. In fact, the reader is reminded to reassess his or her expectations and discoveries continually as the conference goes on. Keeping a sourcebook, log, diary, or plan is useful for some people, although it tends o restrain others. To be sure, participants may have different ways of using a planning sheet or outline like the one depicted in Figure 1. Some prefer to jot down thoughts, while others find it more profitable to list the goals that they are attempting to accomplish. For still others, such procedures sound restrictive. Nevertheless, thinking in these terms will at least afford direction to one's efforts.

If you have kept a contact list from previous years (successful conference consumers usually do), a quick memo or telephone call before the conference to those with whom you would like to reestablish contact—for whatever reason—helps. It is well worth the effort because it prevents leaving such contacts to chance. There will be enough time and moments for chance occurrences.

I suggest that the participant list each category of the sample conference planning sheet depicted in Figure 1 (for example, "people I want to meet," "Problems I am trying to solve") on a separate sheet so that he or she has room for ideas that arise during the conference and for strategies that were not formulated in advance. In fact, the sample conference planning sheet could serve as the framework for a workbook for use by individuals or groups in training sessions for conference consumption either at home before the conference or at an initial workshop preceding conference sessions. Such a workbook might prove particularly useful to a graduate class or other group, such as a special meeting of state affiliate members, in planning for the conference. Moreover, support groups developed through self-initiated effort at the conference may be able to synergistically help one another in planning and strategizing such efforts.

Conference designers can use such a planning aid to organize conference sessions and thereby help conference goers strategize the conference experience, learn how to learn from the conference, and pinpoint or locate resources and contacts. Interim sessions could be held as progress checks to air and deal with frustrations or to devise strategies and develop solutions to problems or blocks encountered. In lieu of specific sessions, a hospitality or other suite could be used to offer assistance of this kind to conferees. Efforts in this direction could be built into an ongoing evaluation system, the results of which were reported on a daily basis to plenary sessions or in a daily bulletin. For example, feedback boxes could be located strategically throughout the conference area as well as in sleeping or eating areas. Feedback sheets that enabled participants to share the joys and frustrations of the conference could be available at each box, but they should also be included in the registration packet. At a minimum, the registration packet should include a planning sheet like that depicted in Figure 1, even if preplanning sessions are not possible. Moreover, if there is a participant program book, it should include a section devoted to conference consuming through individual scheduling.

Networking, the building of support groups, and the maximizing of human contacts as resources are important ingredients that conference planners should keep in mind. Some conference planners have gone so far as to sponsor a matching roommate service. Operating on principles similar to those of dating services (or perhaps a more palatable comparison is educational brokering), this approach seeks to match people with similar interests as roommates for the duration of the conference. Introduction of the computer into conference planning efforts should facilitate such efforts and perhaps even expand them into a resource-type directory of participants. Such information could be used by conference goers (including commuters) in pinpointing resources and in developing networking systems for use both at the conference and afterwards.

This consideration brings the discussion to another central point: The successful conference experience tends to exert its effects well after the conference itself is over. Unfortunately, good ideas, thoughts, new information, and resource contacts all too often dissipate when a participant returns from the conference "high" to the realities of professional life. Even so, this development is usually within some control by the conference consumer. Devising strategies to optimize postconference transfer, implementation, and application of learning as well as nurturing the growth of professional relationships conceived at the conference are all part of the conference consumer stance—in attitude as well as in action. Conference planners would do well to organize mid-conference or end-of-conference sessions to help organize and catalyze such efforts.

Whether these efforts are on an individual basis or part of a group effort, certain essentials can be covered. For example, conference contacts can be organized by who they are, why they are important, what mailing list they belong on, and whether a networking system can be developed. A conference provides the opportunity to develop a resource file of professional contacts and relationships. The resources in this file can be particularly vital in helping to energize and sometimes to strategize one's efforts to transfer and implement good ideas, thoughts, and new information after a conference. Action steps taken at a conference, particularly with the support of others, are helpful later.

The notion of goal setting accompanied by determined action steps is clearly an important ingredient in successful conference consumption.

However, perhaps the main key to optimum conferencing lies in blending such goal-setting and action steps with a go-with-the-flow type of stance in attitude as well as in action. Despite good planning, it is important—as the saying goes—not to confuse the map with the territory. As any good explorer knows, goals and guidelines, maps and plans are important, but they can be counterproductive if they are allowed to obscure the many unexpected tributary possibilities on the journey.

A situation that often occurs is one in which one is invited to go to dinner or for a drink with a group of people. Sometimes people just want to get away from a conference; other times, the invitation results from a lingering postsession discussion. It is not difficult to make the choice to leave a conference for a short period of time in the second case. However, even in the case when people want simply to get away, the informal relaxed atmosphere and context can produce some interesting contacts or discussion. One must determine for oneself if it is worth the time. One must also be prepared just to relax and enjoy the event. One does not want to force others into shop talk or to be angry that one has preferred an ongoing session to small talk. In any event, anger does little to cultivate the good relationships that may have been one's reason for leaving with the group in the first place.

How does one deal with such conflicts, which in psychological terms are referred to as "approach-approach" conflicts? Here is one suggestion: Go to the room where the session that is exerting a gravitational pull on you is being held. If need be, arrange to meet the group at the restaurant or wherever it is planning to meet. If you go before the session is scheduled to begin, you can sometimes spot the serious session consumer. This person, notepad or tape recorder in hand, can often be found sitting at the front of the room ready for the session to begin. Approach this individual; explain that you are unable to attend the session and that you would like to meet with him or her at some designated time and place to learn not only about the presentation but also about any discussion and social dynamics that transpired. In order to make it mutually beneficial, offer to share what you have learned from your group adventure and any contacts that you have made. It is also helpful to share this individual's name and activities with the group. Perhaps the opportunity to exchange business or professional cards will arise. In this way, both a networking system and a learning community are being propagated; in the process, participants can be transformed from conference attenders into conference consumers. Just planting a seed or even thinking or behaving in such a synergistic manner can stimulate thought processes and catalyze proactive behavior on the part of other conference participants. A beneficial spin-off generated from such a move is that both you and the group have made a new contact.

There are other strategies for dealing with approach-approach conflicts, particularly when the conflict is between attending a specific session and doing something else—whatever that might be. The organizers of many large conferences now sell tapes of the sessions; in such cases you can buy a tape if all else fails. Many people prefer to contact someone who went to the session. Such contact can be accomplished informally by random queries addressed to people in passing, during social functions, or at other gathering places. Another strategy is to post a message on a bulletin board (most conferences have one) indicating that you would like to talk with someone who attended the session. Another, more direct strategy, of course, is to contact the presenter via a message on the bulletin board or directly, if you can locate where the presenter is staying. For local presenters, the conference` planning committee may be able to give you an office or a home telephone number.

A special note might be placed on the bulletin board to find others who are interested in similar ideas or activities. Notes provide a successful way to reach out to other conference participants—whether as jogging partners, as people dealing with similar professional problems. In general, the question of how one spends one's time and with whom one spends it are critical decision points at a conference. Thinking this question through in advance helps, but one should also be prepared to deal with unanticipated circumstances.

At an international conference or at a conference attended by international visitors it is usually profitable to spend some time making contact with participants who may live continents away. Despite the advances of modern telecommunications, these conference goers will be harder to reach later. Exchanging addresses, writing a follow-up letter upon one's return home, and keeping selected international participants on a mailing list are all useful ways of developing a worldwide network of colleagues.

The myriad of serendipitous and unexpected findings and occurrences coupled with the variety of planned activities offered at large conferences sometimes leads to feelings of frustration or even helplessness, particularly for first-time conference goers. Although veterans can experience information overload just as well as newcomers, the feeling of being overwhelmed or frustration at not being able to do it all seems to be more acute for first-time conference goers. Sheer size, information overload, lack of direction or support can cause discomfort that manifests itself as withdrawal. It is not at all unusual to find a fair number retreating to their hotel rooms or even to the rest rooms. The presence of cliques at some conferences can aggravate the situation. Despite these problems, a consumer attitude can prevail over such frustrations and allow participants to view conferences as opportunities to learn more about themselves.

It may be helpful for conference goers and conference planners to focus on this withdrawal response, which occurs far more often than we realize. Of course, conferees sometimes plan, even welcome, hibernation for a variety of reasons, and this discussion in no way intends to discourage such a choice if it is made in the interest of healthy recuperation and restoration. However, for some such behavior is a sign of feeling left out. These individuals are lonely and fearful. Such participants typically report feelings of loneliness, sadness, fear, or anger that result in their retreating from the situation. As one participant put it: "If I really think about it, the whole situation reminds me of my previous behaviors in trying unsuccessfully to become part of a group. A sense, real or perceived, of rejection leads to feelings of isolation and aloneness, which in turn affect self-esteem and insecurity and can lead to despair and a little depression." Another conferee emphasized: "Sometimes I have to push myself and just take the step. I tell myself not to hide and not to just cope but to overcome this block."

The block that this participant describes can act as a strong barrier to full participation as a conference consumer. These are the kinds of issues— both external and internal—that one must confront if one is fully to benefit from the potential learning experiences offered by a conference, particularly if the conference is a large one. As the next section of this chapter suggests, there may be a whole host of conference-consuming competencies, including perhaps some social ones. Some conference goers find it helpful to sit in the lobby, to mill around the exhibit area, or to stay near the registration desk or the message center. These are usually the action spots where things tend to happen, even without one's taking the initiative.

The importance of developing both contacts and support structures before, during, and after the conference should be clear. The most critical element is the support structure that one can develop while at the conference. Participants form such a support structure by identifying a few new friends (Boucouvalas and Brysh-Cooke, 1982). The formation of a support group helps participants to reach conference goals. The basic idea is to create a synergistic effort in which participants help one another as well as themselves.

The potential of such a support group depends on the creative efforts of its participants. The members of these informal groups note the other members goals and strategies (as well as the ways and places at which they can be reached while at the conference and at home) so that each person can be actively looking out for the others. It is advisable to include in the group new participants or individuals not previously included. Although it is sometimes more secure and comfortable to spend much time with the group with which one came to the conference, it is preferable, because it is more productive, to disperse and form different support groups. Then, either during the conference or back at home, one can compare notes and multiply the possible learning derivatives. Reflecting over the years on earlier conference-going habits, one conference consumer stated: "The first conference I attended was regional in nature, so I tended to stick with the local people whom I knew. Boy, was that a mistake! I can see how a group mind-set can interfere with maximum benefit that may be derived from a conference. Now

I prefer to go it alone. I'm still friendly with such colleagues—but I find it more expanding not to stick so close. We can build opportunities for that at another time."

An equally important challenge (and another potential block) is to recognize conference consumers and distinguish them from those who attend a conference either just to get away from work or merely to "party." Although it may be possible to learn some social skills from such attenders, it is highly unlikely that one would want to include them in a support group.

In general, newcomers, particularly students, present such unique concerns as to warrant a more concerted focus than I have room for here. Consequently, Meyer devotes the whole of Chapter Five to an examination of the unique problems of first-time participants. While veteran conference goers (particularly at an annual-type conference held by a professional association) sometimes face the problem of overload, they more often get bored. Such individuals may need a different kind of support structure or an alternative strategy or approach to conference consumption. Some longtime conference goers opt to leave the conference before it is over. Others use the time and locale for rest and relaxation and even bring their families with them. Still other conference consumers have devised strategies for exploring, visiting and conducting interviews with people in selected agencies, institutions, and organizations in the area consistent with their professional roles; while these individuals may leave the conference site, they use the conference trip and geographical locale as a valuable learning opportunity.

Of the "veterans" who choose to stay at the conference site, some use the opportunity to catalyze or conclude collaborative writing or research efforts or to seek manuscript review and feedback from colleagues. Others take the initiative in organizing "rump sessions" on a variety of problems and issues of personal concern, often in nightcap sessions held in a bar or hotel room. To avoid the clatter and distraction of a coffee shop breakfast, others hold early morning meetings in their rooms with the assistance of room service. Still others become involved in the politics and planning of present and future conferences. Again, the possibilities are open to the creative energies of the conference consumer who thinks proactively rather than reactively.

Conference Consuming Competencies

Although discussions of conference consumption are still in their infancy, it does not seem premature to begin to explore the notion of conference-consuming competencies. Although more systematic research and analysis will be needed, we might begin to delineate the knowledge, skills, and attitudes that seem helpful in becoming a conference consumer. At a minimum, such an effort could challenge researchers to examine the idea systematically, perhaps it could also encourage conference planners as well as educators to organize sessions and devise activities aimed at helping people to learn how to become better conference consumers. Certainly, much can be gleaned from the literature on the skills of self-directed inquiry (for example, Knowles, 1975; Brookfield, 1985). Peters (1980) moves us in the direction of becoming self-directed conference goers.

The literature on experiential learning should also be helpful, as should the literature on goal setting and prioritizing. Knowledge of how to tap into material and human resources and of how to manage one's time is also useful. The competencies of conference consumption are a complex issue that calls for an understanding of the whole repertoire of knowledge, skills, and attitudes involved in lifelong learning—learning from human and material resources and from experience. One little-discussed competency is that of social skills, which are critical to conference consumption. This is an area that warrants further research and inquiry. As one colleague remarked recently, "Some people just seem to be able to slip right into a group conversation so easily. I don't know whether they emanate charisma, or a 'presence,' or what, but they flow easily among 'strangers.' That's a definite skill or strength that can make a big difference in conference consumption."

Conference Consuming: A Challenge

In this chapter, I have offered a number of challenges to conference goers—neophytes and veterans alike—as well as to conference planners. We must explore the issue of learning how to learn from conferences. We must mature from the reactive role of conference attender to the proactive role of conference consumer. I have urged practitioners to help themselves and each other in this regard. Educators, employers, and community workers can all contribute to this process of educating people to become better conference consumers.

Conference designers and planners are in a particularly strategic position to catalyze such efforts. I have suggested hosting sessions to help participants plan their conference experience and to apply conference learnings or insights to their own situations. Continuous thought and action should be given to devising means of involving participants and forming networking systems. At a minimum, the participant program book or the registration materials should be devoted in part to encouraging conference consumption.

Researchers must become involved or encourage others to become involved in exploring this subject area. Of course, systematic inquiry is needed if we are to determine whether certain competencies in knowledge, skill, or attitude enable participants to become conference consumers. Generating a solid knowledge base in this area could greatly benefit efforts to train or educate people in conference consumption. Not to be overlooked is the role that a variety of social skills may play in this process. As I have indicated most of the research on why and how a person decides to go to a conference has been done by and for those who market conferences. The findings of the research that I suggest could help practitioners learn how to make better choices. Moreover, systematic inquiry into how a variety of individuals successfully strategize for conference consumption and application of conference learnings could help considerably to flesh out educational efforts in this regard.

Finally, it has not been my intent to communicate that consuming, as to opposed to attending, a conference is always better or more advantageous. Rather, the intended message is that a conference consumer makes deliberate choices based on a thoughtful analysis and review of personal needs and goals. There may be times when a conference consumer will choose to attend the conference in a reactive manner, but that choice is usually an exception to typical behavior.

References

Boucouvalas, M., and Brysh-Cooke, C. "Making a National Conference an Adult Learning Experience for You." *Lifelong Learning: The Adult Years,* 1982, *6* (3), 8–11.

Brookfield, S. (Ed.). *Self-Directed Learning: From Theory To Practice.* New Directions for Continuing Education, no. 25. San Francisco: Jossey-Bass, 1985.

Cell, E. *Learning to Learn from Experience.* Albany, N.Y. : SUNY Press, 1984.

Knowles M. S. *Self-Directed Learning: A Guide for Teachers and Learners.* New York: Association Press, 1975.

Knowles, M. S. *The Modern Practice of Adult Education.* (2nd ed.) New York: Cambridge, 1980.

Nadler, L. and Nadler, Z. *The Conference Book.* Houston: Gulf, 1977.

Peters, T. "Become a Self-Directed Conference Goer." *The Learning Connection,* 1980, *1* (2), 2–5.

Marcie Boucouvalas is assistant professor of adult education at the Northern Virginia Graduate Center of Virginia Polytechnic Institute and State University.

Students and newcomers must consider how to become part of the professional community while still developing an understanding of the profession.

Maximizing the Conference Experience for First-Time Participants

Susan Meyer

How do newcomers work toward establishing a professional identity in a field while they are still developing their knowledge of that field? This question can be answered by an analysis of the development of a professional identity through the participation of graduate students and other newcomers in conference activities.

As Boucouvalas makes clear in Chapter Four, all conference attendees have an agenda, although this agenda may not be clearly established beforehand. Whether it is to renew professional relationships, to develop new relationships, to test a new theory, to report on research, or simply to catch up or get away for a few days, we all approach a conference with some preconceived notion of what we hope to achieve. For the newcomer or graduate student, active participation in a conference—development of the learning-community described elsewhere in this volume—is somewhat more complex. How does the newcomer become part of a learning community or establish such a community? How does the newcomer become known to her or his peers and to those whom she or he hopes will help to shape her or his professional growth? How, in short, does one

P. J. Ilsley (Ed.). *Improving Conference Design and Outcomes.* New Directions for Continuing Education, no. 28. San Francisco: Jossey-Bass, December 1985.

develop an agenda for becoming a professional while still negotiating unfamiliar and uncharted territory? All this is basic to the issue of developing a professional identity and some degree of recognition in the new field, that is, professional socialization.

Professional Socialization

Becoming socialized into a field is an essential part of a student's preparation. Classroom learning transmits philosophy, theory, and technique, but it does not sufficiently expose a student to a field's ethos. Some form of experiential learning complementing classroom education helps a student become socialized into a field through controlled experiences and guided participatory observation. The conference is an excellent arena for participatory observation. Here, the student can test the new professional role in limited, relatively protected circumstances and begin to feel like a member of the profession.

In discussing professional socialization, Singer (1982, p. 47) points out that "joining a profession invariably involves a socialization process, which profoundly affects students' lives; that this process takes place in the context of students' adult development and in the light of students' experience of self as they essay various roles involved in being both a student and a fledgling member of the field."

Professional socialization is intrinsic to development of a professional self-concept. It embodies exploratory behavior—trying out different aspects of the professional role and establishing personal norms for the conduct of one's professional life. In a discussion of his theoretical paradigm for career development as implementation of self-concept, Super (1981) states that work provides a focus for personality organization for most individuals and that satisfaction is related to the degree to which a career represents implementation of self-concept. He describes the process of implementing self-concept as "a synthesis and compromise process in which the self-concept is a product of the interaction of inherited aptitudes, neural and endocrine makeup, opportunity to play various roles, and evaluations of the extent to which the results of role playing meet with the approval of superiors and fellows" [p. 37]. It is at conferences that the newcomer may find the first opportunity to try the new role outside the classroom and receive feedback from a wide variety of new and experienced professionals.

The process of developing a professional identity may be somewhat more complicated in continuing education for two reasons. First, the field seems to attract a large number of career changers, so the newcomer may often be involved in breaking or modifying old professional ties while developing new ones. Second, the field is extremely diverse; it encompasses professionals working in settings ranging from community centers or social service agencies to major corporations or universities, and it includes practitioners, counselors, professors, and many individuals who combine several of these roles. Thus, a conference may provide one of the few opportunities to interact with large groups of individuals who clearly define themselves as continuing educators and who are gathered together to devote time solely to the concerns of continuing education.

Conference Participation

The student or newcomer has three main resources to maximize his or her involvement in a conference: faculty and peer contacts, making a presentation at the conference, and volunteering to work on the conference. These resources can be used separately or in combination. Although all three will be touched on in this chapter, my central focus will be the role of the volunteer, which seems at once to be one of the most overlooked and one of the most meaningful educational tools.

Using Relationships. Good relationships between faculty members and students can be used beneficially at a conference. Faculty interested in the professional growth of their students take time to encourage students to attend conferences, suggest sessions that may be most beneficial, and assist students to meet others in the field. This effort need not be a time-consuming task for the professor but a few minutes well invested that provide long-term benefits for the student. Newcomers meet other newcomers, share their interests and experiences, and return to the classroom richer for the experience. Some examples of the beginnings of learning communities that resulted from peer meetings at conferences, garnered from discussions with recent conference attendees, follow.

A student from Florida and a student from New York meet at one conference and discover they have similar research interests. They meet again at a second conference, and their discussion with another group of students proves to be the high point of an otherwise very dull meeting and possibly the springboard for joint presentations in the future.

Students from two different programs at the same university are introduced at a conference and arrange to have dinner together. As a result, they develop relationships that might not have otherwise been possible with such different on-campus schedules.

A newcomer from Alaska meets two newcomers from New York. The friendship that develops brightens the free time during the conference. It becomes a regular reunion every two years and the basis for an expanding network that includes counselors, continuing educators, and program administrators who share professional information and contacts.

A group of students from the same program meet to review the conference agenda and arrange to cover the largest number of sessions possible and exchange notes afterwards.

The incidents just described might easily happen without outside intervention. Students find it easy to develop relationships with other students—if they can find them—although this may be less true for other newcomers. At the same time, faculty members can do a few simple things to enhance their students' conference experience, especially as it involves developing relationships with experienced professionals. Often, faculty automatically do these things, but students should feel free to request faculty assistance. First, faculty can try to identify all students who are attending a conference and facilitate their travel arrangements or suggest how they might coordinate in order to travel together (inexpensively, if possible). Second, once at the conference, faculty can take a few minutes to be sure that all the students know each other. After the introductions have been performed, the group can make its own decisions about how—or if—it will function. Often, students from large programs have never met on campus. The experience of returning home after spending all one's free time alone at a conference only to find that others from your program were there is less than pleasant and easy to avoid. Third, if colleagues from other programs have students in attendance, faculty can arrange for the two groups to meet simply by introducing the "natural organizers" from each program. Again, the exchange of perspectives can strengthen a program as well as provide a resource network for the students in it. Fourth, faculty can make an effort to perform at least one introduction and try to be available to students for part of one general reception or social hour in order to help them meet colleagues. Last, faculty can join students for one meal or evening's relaxation. The absence of on-campus time constraints and the relatively informal atmosphere make it easier for shy students to get to know their faculty.

All these activities provide opportunities for modeling. Just as some companies ask new employees to shadow someone with more experience as a means of teaching the actual on-the-job activities, students can use conferences to investigate aspects of the professional role. One student beginning her second year of conference attendance noted that she was finally beginning to feel more relaxed and accepted. She was beginning to recognize faces from previous conferences and to feel part of the milieu. She commented that she had been having difficulty envisioning herself in a professional role but, after several successful conference experiences, that she was finally beginning to feel, "I can do that!"

Making a Presentation. One way in which a newcomer can begin to be part of a conference is by making a presentation. Graduate students and newcomers occasionally have difficulties moving into the role of conference presenter. They may not feel that they have anything original or profound to say. Once again, faculty support is extremely important in this area.

Preparing and presenting papers or workshop sessions provides invaluable experience to the student or newcomer, both in developing research skills and in developing confidence and public presentation skills. Some newcomers have difficulty attending a conference without a set role.

They find the role of observer uncomfortable when it is separated from some structure for participation. The role of presenter gives a context within which the new professional may begin to feel comfortable sharing ideas and observations with others.

Details of how to prepare and deliver papers can be found elsewhere. The focus here is on how to become comfortable with the role of presenter and on how to use presentations as professional development. As with any other speaking or writing, the best first-time conference presentation builds on the familiar. This fact extends beyond topic choice to format and selection of appropriate conferences to attend.

Topic Selection. Before planning a presentation, the student or newcomer should engage in a little market research. What is the theme of the conference? Who attends? What formats are possible? Are all sessions paper presentations, or are discussions, group exercises, or symposia alternatives to consider? What kinds of topics have a high likelihood of acceptance? Once this information has been obtained from professors, attendees of previous conferences, or colleagues, the new presenter can begin to fit specific ideas into an appropriate framework.

Schoolwork or current projects at work provide an excellent source of topics that can be developed into presentations. A paper originally written for a course may fit well with the theme of a particular conference. A master's thesis or doctoral dissertation may provide concepts that can be expanded into presentations. Any topic that draws on the familiar may be the best place to start, as the presenter is then likely to feel most comfortable and have the widest range of information readily at hand.

For the student, using school assignments increases feelings of competence. For the career changer, using material based on earlier professional experiences may increase a feeling of identification with the new field. This idea is not dissimilar to the concept of skills transferability, which serves as the mainstay of most career counseling interventions for individuals changing careers or reentering the labor market.

Format. When newcomers plan their first presentation, they may find truth in the old adage that there is strength in numbers. Most conferences provide for symposia or joint presentations, and these formats may be less anxiety provoking for first-time presenters. Many conferences devote sections of the program to work in progress or to student presentations. At these sections, individuals present papers, have an opportunity to share ideas that may not yet be fully developed, and receive feedback that can guide them in further study or research. Such sections provide a somewhat protected atmosphere.

While a joint presentation has the advantage of built-in moral support, there are several issues to consider before selecting this format. Joint paper presentations or special sessions devoted to related papers by individuals who have not previously met or prearranged the presentation are relatively straightforward, as each presenter need only be responsible for getting through her or his own material and answering related questions. Workshops or cofacilitated discussion are more complex and require considerable advance preparation. Because the presenters are interdependent and working in a counseling mode, they must spend some time anticipating and understanding group dynamics. They must come to prior agreement about points to stress in the discussion, about which facilitator is most comfortable with which issues, and about how they will share leadership and make decisions as the session progresses. Individuals who do not have counseling or group leadership experience may not wish to begin with this relatively risky and self-revealing form of presentation.

Planning and giving a presentation provide an opportunity to test or adapt many professional skills. The inexperienced new professional can use this opportunity to develop public speaking skills that he or she will need in both classroom and administrative roles. The career changer can use this opportunity to adapt presentation skills developed in other fields to the style, issues, and areas of concern to the new field. Both students and career changers can use conference presentations to begin to develop a professional voice.

Volunteering. A graduate student or other career changer often uses a conference as a means of developing a new professional identity. For many, this will not be their first career. The prospective adult educator is also an adult learner. Thus, for the adult education graduate student, conference participation as a volunteer can be a valuable educational tool.

Citing growth needs as one motivation for volunteering, Ilsley and Niemi (1981) go on to describe these needs: "Growth needs refer to learning, development, and a striving to reach full potential. This view corresponds with current thinking in the area of human development, notably the belief that a person's growth continues throughout life. The need for new experiences is tantamount to the thirst for adventure and the urge to try new activities and take risks [p. 87]. Jordaan (1963) points out that exploratory behavior is essential to career development. For the individual who is seeking to enter a new field, volunteer experience provides the opportunity for growth and exploration, basic components of the move towards establishment in a profession.

Volunteer Participation

Working on a conference has benefits both for the student and the faculty sponsor if this participation is well planned and thought through in advance. Most obviously, it helps the student to understand the scope of the conference. It gives the student an opportunity to work closely not only with his or her own faculty but also with faculty of other institutions involved in the conference. If the volunteer is involved in scheduling or choosing presentations, the experience may provide the chance to work with people who have previously only been names in texts. The preestablished role allows even the least confident individual to plunge into a conference with a feeling of belonging and a means for interacting freely with other participants.

For faculty, encouraging student participation has rewards beyond the obvious source of cheap, generally malleable labor. Student enthusiasm is contagious, and it can revitalize one's own sometimes flagging energy and enthusiasm. Students contribute fresh ideas. A newcomer may see something that eludes the more seasoned practitioner or bring fresh approaches from his or her own professional experience. Student volunteers at a recent career conference were able to identify the source of a traffic flow problem that had eluded the conference organizers for two years simply by repositioning a central row of tables and the registration table.

Volunteer Participation as Self-Directed Learning. To derive maximum benefit from involvement in conference activities, planners and participants might best think of the volunteer experience as a self-directed learning opportunity. Even before eliciting the assistance of student volunteers, the conference organizer should map out clearly what will be expected of volunteers and what educational benefits are inherent in the experience before, during, and after the conference. What activities does each volunteer prefer? What skills does each volunteer hope to develop through participation in this event?

How can conference participation be classified as self-directed learning? Both Knowles (1980) and Brookfield (1984) include these elements in their definitions of self-directed learning: The learner makes decisions about goals, the learner identifies resources for learning, and the learner chooses and implements learning strategies. If conference planners keep these specifications in mind, the conference can become a self-directed learning experience.

As the student decides to volunteer, he or she must establish clear learning goals. Discussion with the conference coordinator will determine whether these goals can be met and provide an opportunity to reach consensus on how to implement individual goals. What specific learning will be accomplished? With whom does the learner wish to interact?

Finally, the learner needs some strategy to reinforce the self-directed learning. Some immediate written record of the conference experience that can be analyzed after some time has elapsed may be the most useful means of documenting learning. Some program planners suggest keeping a conference log. This strategy is also often used in experiential education as part of fulfilling a learning contract. The learner records reactions as close to events as possible and later reviews the contents of the log and comments on the immediate reactions. Lists of skills are available that can help learners identify what they hope to develop or simply help them to organize their thinking in the conference log.

Broadening Networks. Volunteer experience helps an individual to try out a new professional role and develop professional relationships. All new professionals share the need to establish links with established professionals. One of the greatest advantages in helping to run a conference is the opportunity to do this. Members of the conference committee can more easily interact with attendees without feeling constrained. The role removes some of the hesitancy that some feel about approaching people whom they do not know. It provides a context within which newcomers can become acquainted with professionals in the field. It also gives others an opportunity to judge the caliber of the volunteer's work. If the conference runs smoothly, that is in part a reflection on the volunteer's competence.

The issue of developing professional relationships may be more pertinent for the female volunteer. A quick look at the roster of volunteers for several conferences clearly establishes that most volunteers are women. That there are more female than male graduate students only partially accounts for this phenomenon. It appears that women are more likely than men are to use volunteer work as a way of establishing themselves in a field. Often, the male graduate student can still simply count on making contacts over a drink at the end of the day. In many fields and professions, women are invited to "join the club" in this way; nevertheless, it is unlikely that nonsexist behavior will soon be adopted universally. Thus, volunteer experiences may provide the only opportunity for modeling for women in some fields. It therefore becomes increasingly important for women to be sure that this volunteer experience goes beyond typing, copying, handling registration, and running errands to include some meaningful interaction with conference attendees.

In this, the conference organizer's support is essential. Women are involved in a wide range of conference activities beginning with typing nametags and ending with selecting the papers to be presented. Availability and logistics sometimes determine the volunteer's level of participation, but just as often the level seems to be strongly influenced by the attitude of the organizer. The organizer who allows volunteers to use their creative abilities and to be full participants in the decision-making process is likely not only to find that dull tasks are handled more rapidly but to find that the whole conference runs much more smoothly. A little bit of challenge goes a long way toward motivating volunteers.

Experiential Learning. As its name suggests, experiential learning is participatory learning. An individual engages in an activity and draws information from the activity that contributes to the learner's store of knowledge. Most generally, the term is used in connection with credit for life experience or some sort of internship or cooperative education program. A well-organized co-op program provides an excellent example of what experiential learning can be at its best and provides clues as to how this process can further professional development through volunteer activities at conferences.

First, each student works with a coordinator to assess professional goals. Then, learning experiences in the form of work placements are selected to form a progression toward those goals. As the student progresses through a work period, weekly seminars give the student an opportunity to analyze and discuss the situation—to identify strengths and weaknesses during the work experience, to analyze problems, and to receive peer and faculty support in any concomitant role transition. At the end of the work period, the student evaluates the experience as a whole and makes plans for new learning. When classroom attendance is not feasible, the ongoing experience can be analyzed and feedback can be provided by means of written logs and learning contracts.

It seems to me that this model has something to offer conference organizers who wish to ensure a meaningful experience for volunteers. Indeed, planning and implementing a conference has been used in some cases as a course activity. Working through goals before beginning the actual conference work may seem time-consuming, but it ensures the volunteer's active participation. The use of a learning contract can help to make the conference a tangible learning experience for volunteers. A simple form on which each volunteer lists his or her goals and expectations can be distributed the first time the group meets. The coordinator might also give volunteers a rough idea of his or her goals and expectations and of the variety of tasks to be done. This clear establishment of mutual goals and understanding of tasks goes a long way toward avoiding misunderstandings of the I-didn't-expect-to-have-to-do-that variety. It also gives the coordinator a chance to assess the reality of everyone's expectations and the likelihood that the group will actually be able to handle the tasks at hand without being overburdened.

Planning for the Involvement of Volunteers. Although the importance of planning has been mentioned several times, it needs to be stated that it is probably the single most important factor in the successful use of volunteers if there is to be an educational experience. Ilsley and Niemi (1981) provide an excellent discussion of the use of volunteers in the context of running long-range programs, and much of the information that they provide is useful to the conference coordinator. These authors remind us that the volunteer needs to experience an assimilation process. For a conference, assimilation and team building must occur within a relatively short period of time. Ideally, volunteers meet together with the coordinator as early in the planning process as possible and begin to learn how they can best work together. The coordinator may need to help group members determine how they can best work together and make use of everyone's talents. The conference planned as part of a program development course certainly best meets this need.

Problem Areas. In preparing this chapter, I spoke with a number of people who had either been volunteers or used volunteers at conferences and collected the following laundry list of complaints. Most of them may sound familiar:

Some volunteers were asked to select one or two assignments that interested them only to be assigned totally unrelated duties. Other volunteers were given no choice of assignment. Volunteers expect their suggestions to be taken seriously. Several complained that their suggestions were ignored until a fresh voice or someone further up in the hierarchy repeated them. The vanishing volunteer was the subject of numerous complaints. There are several categories of vanishing volunteer. First, there is the person who misses all the planning sessions but shows up for the main event, thereby needing lengthy explanations and in general taking up more time than he or she is likely to return. Second, there is the person who attends all the planning sessions faithfully, then disappears. Often, this person has a key assignment. Third, there is the person who disappears inexplicably once activities are under way and reappears just in time for thanks and congratulations.

Overwork seems difficult to avoid, especially when the volunteer staff is small. Several volunteers reported leaving conferences without any idea of what went on most of the time because they were so overburdened with behind-the-scenes maintenance chores. Lack of recognition or thanks is a rare occurrence, but occasionally a coordinator slips up. Even a few words of public recognition or a follow-up note suffice to ensure future support. At the same time, the volunteer who feels that his or her mere presence is a gift beyond price has been a thorn in the side of many a coordinator. Finally, sexist behavior runs the range from stereotypical assignment of duties, to bemoaning the lack of male volunteers while watching female volunteers carry heavy equipment, to decrying men as generally inferior to women.

This list may seem overly simplistic or familiar, yet these are errors we all can make, regardless of how much conference planning or volunteer experience we have. It serves to emphasize the need to plan, to know the people with whom one is working, to understand the task at hand, and to maintain good channels of communication if the conference experience is to be successful for all involved.

Making a Conference Work

How do graduate students and newcomers work toward establishing a professional identity in a field while they are still developing their knowledge of that field? In the final analysis, they must begin to do the things that established professionals do. They must use conference time by becoming active participants as Boucouvalas describes the process in Chapter Four.

However, students and newcomers must be more responsible for those who have been in the field for some time for taking the initiative in developing professional relationships. They must be willing to run the risk of feeling awkward or foolish as they approach strangers to introduce themselves or as they get up to present a paper for the first time. The greater the risk-taking behavior, the greater the rewards.

Faculty and seasoned professionals can help students and newcomers simply by remembering what it is like to be in a transitional stage. Most theorists assign career exploration behavior to adolescence, and although this exploration may occur much later in life, it still seems to evoke all the emotions of adolescence. Who does not remember, with lingering discomfort, the uncertainties of trying out roles for the first time, of trying to become part of a group, of trying to understand norms and modify one's actions so as to fit them?

Much of my counseling is done with career changers, and I, too, have changed careers more than once. The idea of trying to fit into a new role is always part of the discussion. If the newcomer recognizes that he or she is in a transition and actively engages in exploratory behavior, career growth or change is easier to manage. By taking an active role in conference activities, especially a clearly delineated role as a volunteer, the newcomer ensures the opportunity for exploration and growth. Faculty, seasoned professionals, and peers who recognize that new roles and situations have an element of risk can all take an extra moment to reach out and include the newcomer. The student or newcomer should remember that, as in adolescence, the awkwardness is a transitory and probably necessary developmental activity and that only repeated experimentation and a variety of experiences create eventual expertise.

References

Brookfield, S. *Adult Learners, Adult Education, and the Community.* New York: Teachers College Press, 1984.

Ilsley, P. J., and Niemi, J. A. *Training and Recruiting Volunteers.* New York: McGraw-Hill, 1981.

Jordaan, J. P. "Exploratory Behavior: The Formulation of Self and Occupational Concepts." In D. Super (Ed.), *Career Development: Self Concept Theory.* New York: College Entrance Examination Board, 1663.

Knowles, M. *The Modern Practice of Adult Education: From Pedagogy to Andragogy.* Chicago: Follett, 1980.

Singer, D. L. "Professional Socialization and Adult Development in Graduate Professional Education." In B. Menson (Ed.), *Building Experiences in Adult Development.* New Directions for Experimental Learning, no. 16. San Francisco: Jossey-Bass, 1982.

Super, D. "A Developmental Theory: Implementing A Self Concept." In D. H. Montross and C. J. Shinkman (Eds.), *Career Development In The 1980's: Theory and Practice.* Springfield, Ill.: Charles C. Thomas, 1981.

Susan Meyer is an independent consultant in the areas of career development, job training and adult learning, in Brooklyn, New York.

If large conferences are too hectic to allow for effective learning,
try residential conferences.

Quality Learning Through Residential Conferences

Michael Collins

This chapter examines the special benefits that accrue from thoughtfully planned short-term residential conferences. A great deal has been written about residential conferences in Europe (Houle, 1971), particularly the remarkable Danish Folk High Schools and the academically focused residential adult education colleges of the United Kingdom. By and large, these programs require a relatively long-term commitment of a year or more, although there are indications that the Danish Folk High Schools are now inclined to offer programs of shorter duration (Titmus, 1981). From the outset, American variations on the European approach to residential continuing education, of which the celebrated Highlander Folk School (Adams, 1975) is an outstanding example, have been characterized by relatively short-term residential educational events.

This chapter is concerned with short-term residential adult education conferences of four to five days duration—approximately the time normally allocated for large-scale national conferences. Where residential continuing education experiences of less than three days (two evenings) are contemplated, one would certainly question whether the distinctive qualities of residential conferences set out in this chapter could be realized. Apart from offering suggestions for enhancing the effectiveness of short-term residential conferences, I will touch lightly on some of the theoretical

P. J. Ilsley (Ed.). *Improving Conference Design and Outcomes.* New Directions
for Continuing Education, no. 28. San Francisco: Jossey-Bass, December 1985.

concepts that justify a serious consideration of this format as a distinctive and very necessary alternative to our typical North American conference.

The distinction that I have drawn between traditional conferences and short-term residential conferences might be challenged on the basis that the traditional conferences also entail a concern with the accommodation of participants over several days. The point to be stressed is that in the case of adult residential programming it is not merely the physical accommodation of participants that is of concern: *Residence itself becomes an integral dimension of the learning experience.*

A very deliberate effort is required on the part of residential conference organizers to engender a shared experience among all participants. Recreational activities, mealtimes, and the layout of living quarters should reflect the communal nature of the residential continuing education experience. In contrast to the determined efficiency of large conferences, which creates a sense of busyness and fleeting contacts among participants, the atmosphere of residential continuing education programs should be homely and practical to encourage face-to-face interaction and unhurried discussion. This by no means precludes careful preparation, but the effects of a residential continuing education conference will be entirely spoilt if the organizers attempt to cram in a tightly packaged program. The preferred orientation is toward interaction among participants in an environment where the pace of events is conducive to reflection on important issues. For a short period, participants of residential conferences are encouraged to "grow older together" (Schutz, 1973) in the same sense that members of a family are able to experience one another. The extent to which this kind of experience can be realized through an emphasis on communal values determines the level of intersubjective understanding among participants. Some measure of intersubjective understanding is necessary if the themes of the conference are to be explored in a more thoroughgoing manner than in our day-to-day taken for granted activities when decisions to act have to be made promptly.

The kind of circumstances alluded to here are not easy to achieve. While some tips and recipes can be offered, it is apparent that short-term residential continuing education conferences call more for planned ambience than for a set of standardized procedures. A major purpose of short-term residential conferences is to provide an alternative to the busyness syndrome and frenetic pace often associated with American conferencing which places the emphasis on efficient planning, needs assessment techniques, public relations, scheduling, tracking, space allocation, formal evaluations, and so on. For organizers of typical conferences, management considerations are paramount. They are usually charged with programming for large numbers of participants drawn from a wide geographic area. While it is true that sessions are often plugged in for special-interest groups, there is rarely sufficient time or an adequate context for the analysis of important issues in anything more than a superficial manner. The challenge for organizers of continuing education residential conferences, then, is to structure a learning environment conducive to careful investigations of relevantly selected topics (that is, pertinent to the commitments of all participants) where typical day-to-day distractions are minimized.

It should be apparent that outcomes cannot be specified beforehand since the intent of the residential experience is to explore difficult practical or policy concerns from a number of perspectives. Accordingly, organizers must be prepared to drop some components of the program and add others, even though the overall focus remains the same. The intent of short-term residential continuing education conferences is to set a scene that allows participants to become the producers or creators of their educational program, not mere consumers.

The success of short-term residential continuing education cannot be judged on the basis of the number of people in attendance. Clearly, the participating group has to be small enough for members to establish their individual identities within it (Houle, 1971). Fifty to sixty participants must be regarded as the maximum for a four- to five-day residential program. If feasible, organizers should opt for a smaller number. There is always a temptation to accept more people in response to enthusiastic applications or pressure from external agencies whose support is important to the program. Organizers have to be firm on this matter. An overlay large group of participants will have a deleterious effect on the program, since it is essential to establish dialogic, face-to-face interaction among participants at the outset. The opening session sets the tone for the democratic manner in which discussion is to be conducted during the entire residential experience. It is essential for the participating group to be small enough that all its members can feel comfortable as discussants (Paterson, 1970).

If successful, the sessions at residential conferences become quite intensive and require the serious engagement of participants. Hence, both the programmatic structure and the physical setting should be such that participants can get away on their own or with companions for periods of reflection necessary to sharpen mental focus. It is not advisable for recreational options to be formally programmed after the manner of conferences in general, but the physical setting should belong to the residential experience. Participants should be drawn to exploring their surroundings free from the kind of interruptions encountered in their usual busy round of day-to-day living. For these reasons, rural or semirural settings are usually preferred by organizers of residential conferences. While it is not necessary for the program to be held in an established residential continuing education center for the benefits of residential education to be realized, organizers should be well acquainted with the location selected and its facilities. However, I am not talking about an idyllic rustic retreat that provides little more than an escape from adult responsibilities. Short-term continuing education conferences are intended to perform a vital function by addressing issues and concerns that are overlooked or inevitably curtailed at typical conferences.

Very much absorbed with problems of advanced technology and systematic planning, continuing educators have tended to deal with matters of technique separately from ethical and practical concerns or as nonnegotiable confrontations between humanistic and technicist interests, even though it is clear that their consequences must overlap. Short-term residential conferences provide a learning environment conducive to careful deliberations where the interrelated human and technical dimensions of selected topics can be explored in a rational manner and the consequences for projects of action and vital decision making can be drawn.

In claiming that residential continuing education provides appropriate contexts for topics of an ethical and practical nature, I am not advocating a naive antitechnology stance. For example, it would be very worthwhile to include demonstrations and hands-on experience of electronic data processing equipment as part of a residential program where engagement with technological hardware and software was accompanied by analysis from participants of technology's practical and ethical aspect. For example, the many influences of computers in the field of adult basic education could be considered, or the implications for the poorer sections of society (from which typical ABE students are drawn) that cannot afford to keep up with the trend. In such circumstances, participants are invited to do more than merely cope or catch up with the technology.

The overall theme or major topic of a short-term residential conference should be selected for its relevance to the leading interests of all prospective participants. In this regard, we can anticipate that participants will be a distinctly homogeneous group. By and large, the purpose of a short-term residential experience is to provide a context in which participants who already share a common concern about an issue can investigate its ramifications as a community. It is quite likely that, in the first instance, the topic will have been identified by individuals who intend to be part of the entire proceedings. In any event, the overall relevance of the topic is the determining factor in attracting participants who can make worthwhile contributions and reap the benefits of a residential program. Detailed formal assessment procedures should be unnecessary. The theme itself will be a good indicator of the kind of resource people who can be approached for programming ideas prior to the conference. In a sense, the importance of the topic, its relevance dimension, is a reliable confirmation that it responds to established needs.

Since active involvement in the process is the key to residential conferences, all reasonable efforts should be made to engage prospective participants in some aspect of preconference planning. In some cases, this may entail little more than asking for suggestions in an informal way. At the same time, it is appropriate to circulate to potential participants short, carefully selected reading materials related to the conference theme. To the extent that active involvement remains a priority throughout the residential learning experience, the program should be regarded as formative rather than predetermined in nature. It is necessary to provide substantial periods of time that have not already been defined by prescheduled events so that participants can assess the directions and emphases of their residential learning experience.

This kind of orientation represents a sharp contrast to the growing hyperrationalization of continuing education program planning, which in its extreme form leaves participants with a passive or puerile role to play in the proceedings. As is the case with the tightly organized activities of Disneyland, participants at many large-scale conferences have become spectators or mere consumers of the programmed events that fill the precisely sequenced daily schedule, not participants in the creation of their own learning experience.

For short-term residential conferences, a deliberate effort should be made not to cram the schedule. Arranging for space in a time and at a location in which participants can reflect on the progress of unfolding events on their own account does not preclude paying attention to housekeeping details, nor does it mean abrogating the facilitative role. It does require confidence that the formal facilitative and organizing roles will become gradually more redundant during the course of the residential experience as participants become better at participating.

Typically, of course, come eventualities can be anticipated due to participants's background in the selected theme and their experience with rational discourse in group settings. These anticipated eventualities, combined with suggestions from potential participants, provide the ingredients of the formal program outline, which, as I have indicated, should not be represented as an unalterable catalogue of procedural imperatives.

Care should be taken not to overdo the residential experience deliberately avoiding the inclination to emulate the veneer and antiseptic conformity of modern convention sites with their built-in nonstop busyness. Mealtimes should be shared by all participants in a relatively leisurely fashion, although we should bear in mind that some people are a little late to start and others are slow to finish. It does not require meticulous preprogramming and formal notification to appreciate that shared mealtimes present an occasion for mulling over the outcomes of the day's learning experience.

It is desirable to be alert to the egalitarian nature of good discussion in which there is no privileged status except where it is bestowed by the group as relevant to the flow of rational discourse. When subject area specialists are invited, they should be urged to take part in the entire residential program so that they are not experienced by others only in their role as expert. This tactic prevents the emergence of two classes of participants; namely, those who know and the rest.

While we can hope for some significant changes in individual perspectives to come about from a residential continuing education experience, the intent is not to plan for general accord as a major outcome. A move toward intersubjective understanding through rational discourse, in which participants experience others' points of view as they investigate aspects of the issue at hand, will identify the bases on which rational decision making can take place. It is apparent that in such a context evaluation by participants is a continuous, integral aspect of the residential learning process, the quality of which is largely their responsibility. For this reason, it is hardly necessary for organizers to design a formal evaluation procedure. As a rule, it is a good idea to have a wrap-up session in which participants can be invited to record impressions of the residential experience that can appear in the written proceedings. The written proceedings can be based on written summaries undertaken by participants throughout the conference.

One useful approach is to use tape recordings as a support for written summaries when compiling formal proceedings. In any event, since it is better for proceedings to be read than to be stored, concision is preferable to compendious accounts. A reasonable amount of time can elapse before formal proceedings are mailed out. They will then come as a reminder to participants, who once again are preoccupied with the habitual activities of their everyday lives, of a distinctive learning experience that has a direct bearing on quality of life.

In view of the complex management problems and increasing costs associated with large-scale conferences, short-term residential conferences are an attractive alternative for continuing educators. Teleconferencing and various sophisticated means of communication may be making it less necessary for large numbers of persons from distant locations to converge on one conference center for the dissemination and exchange of information pertinent to their field of interest. However, I have made a case for short-term residential conferences on the basis that they enable us to address critical issues that require careful analysis. Many of these issues emerge from the growing divergence between advances in technology and the solutions available to meet the difficult practical problems associated with these advances. Short-term residential conferences can provide a suitable educative context for purposeful, in-depth analysis of the practical and ethical problems arising from an advanced technological society that still aspires to participatory democracy. Even if it does not offer an entirely new direction for continuing education, the notion of short-term residential adult education merits our serious attention as a practical alternative to large-scale conferencing.

References

Adams, F., *Unearthing Seeds of Fire: The Idea of Highlander.* Winston-Salem, N.C.: Blair, 1975.

Houle, C. O. *Residential Continuing Education.* Syracuse, N.Y.: Syracuse University Publications in Continuing Education, 1971.

Paterson, R. W. K. "The Concept of Discussion: A Philosophical Approach." *Studies in Adult Education,* 1970, 2(1), 28–50.

Schutz, A. *Collected Papers.* Vol. 3: *The Problem of Social Reality.* The Hague: Nijhoff, 1973.

Titmus, C. *Strategies for Adult Education: Practices in Western Europe.* Chicago: Follett, 1981.

Michael Collins is assistant professor of adult education at the University of Saskatchewan. Previously he was assistant professor of adult education at Kansas State University.

To determine the trends for conference planning, we need only examine our past successes.

Analyzing Trends in Conference Design

William A. Draves

Conferences of the future will probably be more exciting, useful, and enjoyable than those of today. At least there is no reason why they should not be more valuable, because several changes in the learning society are taking place right now that will propel us to better conferencing. Four major forces will provide the major influences on all adult learning in the next decade, and they affect conferences and meetings as well. are friendly competition, appeals to the emotions, demands for quality, and increased research and development.

First, the competition will become more friendly. Right now most conference planners offer the same kind of format. The competition that began two years ago, when hospitals, museums, and zoos became conference purveyors, will continue to grow. The increase in programs and available formats, which range from weekend courses to video cassettes, means that adult learners will have a greater variety of learning opportunities from which to choose. Seen from the perspective of the 160 million adult learners out there, this is not competition at all but the liberation of learning. For an adult learner, this is an increasingly exciting time when information about anything from the inner workings of the brain to life in outer space is available in any number of formats from just about any institution in the community, ranging from the college to the church.

P. J. Ilsley (Ed.). *Improving Conference Design and Outcomes.* New Directions
for Continuing Education, no. 28. San Francisco: Jossey-Bass, December 1985.

Conference planners need to reverse their thinking and view the changing adult learning scene not from the point of view of competition but from the perspective of learners. Doing so can be liberating for adult learning programs that choose to develop new strategies to take advantage of the liberation of learning.

We could generously compare ourselves to American Telephone and Telegraph, which recently lost its monopoly on telephone service. Those of us in formal adult education organizations have had a monopoly on adult and continuing education. AT&T is now looking for new avenues for growth and development, and that is precisely what adult educators need to do.

As as result of this diversification, the competition down the block may specialize in an area that differs from ours. Thus, while there will always be competition, it will not always be head to head, as it is today, and the competition will become friendlier. We may even begin talking or even cooperating on a limited basis with organizations that do not directly compete with us.

Second, we will appeal to the emotions. Today the average American is subject to 1,700 advertising impressions a day, five times as many as the average Frenchman. But, our heads can only hold so much information, and as consumers we turn to what we believe and to our own feelings about products and services (Ries and Trout, 1981).

Business recognized this fact years ago and began marketing less with information and more with emotional appeal. We in adult education are far behind, but we can easily catch up. Our catalogues and brochures are full of cognitive information about conference learning opportunities. Generally we fail to acknowledge that people attend conferences for emotional reasons, such as meeting other people, having a good time, and gaining self-respect. People do attend conferences for less than cerebral reasons, and that is not only a reality but a healthy reality. We need to appeal more to our feelings in promoting our programs. This life-style approach will make our programs better, increase the effectiveness of our marketing, and position our conferences in the minds of the professionals whom we attempt to serve.

Third, participants' expectations will go up suddenly and dramatically, and this will have serious implications for programs that are not of the highest quality. The discussion group and the flip chart will soon pale for learners who have become familiar with these effective but overused learning formats.. Participants will grow discontented with presenters who provide substance without style. And, their feelings will border on hostility for the presenters who have style without substance. We can no longer provide an intellectual Johnny Carson show for adult learners tired of television. We have to become more sophisticated in our use of audiovisuals, music, room setup, video equipment, and participant involvement. And, we have to train our teachers better.

Fourth, research in the field will grow. We are part of the information business, currently the fourth largest growth industry in the country. Most companies in high-growth industries spend up to 15 percent of their budgets on research. Adult learning budgets do not allow 5 percent, much less 15 percent, for research and development.

Two things will happen in this area. First, planners will view market research as part of their jobs, not as something that professors do for them once every five years. With the sophisticated and inexpensive research tools that business has developed, conference planners can conduct cost-effective, action-oriented market research on an ongoing basis. Second, planners will increasingly use outside consultants to provide with accurate information and counsel on specific aspects of programming. For example, the Learning Resources Network (LERN) has established itself as the leading research organization for noncredit programming by conducting nationwide surveys and passing the information on to local programs for a fraction of the original cost.

In summary, an increasingly wide spectrum of organizations will be involved in adult learning programming in the coming few years, but there will be an equal number of opportunities for the programs that already provide classes for adults. The key will be to reorient ourselves to the new and emerging environment, cut loose outmoded programs, and engage in new growth. The most striking result of the major changes in adult learning on conferences of the future is that conferences will become more distinct from each other, not just in content but in format, benefits, and atmosphere. This diversification will be exciting for attendees. Finally, all four major directions in learning—increased choice for learners, life-style marketing, demands for quality, and research into successful education practices—require conference planners to make their meetings specialized, different, and aimed at a specific market segment.

The Conference of the Future

As conferences diversify, consumers will need to isolate the most important factors involved in attending a conference. These factors include purpose, physical setting, subject, format, and presentation techniques.

Purpose. Market segmentation is occuring in every aspect of life. One conference cannot be everything to everybody. Conferences will therefore diversify in purpose. Everyone knows that some conferences today have excellent keynote speakers and poor workshops, while others have poor general sessions and great workshops. Still others have poor sessions and many people milling about in the halls conducting important back room business, making contacts, generating leads, and meeting people. Conference promoters still do not openly acknowledge the weaknesses in their conferences and seek to play on their strengths. The conference that is really a networking opportunity with poor workshops still pretends that it has good workshops and dutifully schedules them every year. Just about every conference has general sessions, workshops, receptions, social activities, exhibits, and individual networking. In the future, some of these activities will be dropped, while others will become more prominent as conference promoters manifestly market their particular conference advantages. Here are some of the purposes in which conferences will specialize:

- The major speaker, the "big picture" outlook
- Awards and recognition for individual participants
- Opportunity for new people to offer ideas and techniques in a workshop setting
- Only the highest-quality workshops by leading experts in the business
- Introductory and basic knowledge and information for people new to the field
- Advanced information for the experienced practitioner
- Business contacts—a place to sell your products or services
- A place to buy products or services
- Networking—a chance to meet individuals one to one, sit down and talk, and get to know one another
- Career advancement—an opportunity to demonstrate your ability or even interview for other jobs
- Prestige opportunities for presenters
- A time to rejuvenate your energies for your job
- A well-deserved vacation provided by the company as a reward for your hard work over the past year
- A social time where the best parties of the year are held.

Obviously one conference can fulfill more than one need for a participant, but the emphasis and distinctions are growing more acute with every conferencing season. For example, in adult and continuing education the near trend for the next five years will be to have fewer workshops of higher quality. Many organizations are now looking to limit the number of presentations and to seek advanced ideas and presenters of high quality.

Five years from now, conference sponsors will increasingly have a relatively focused and narrow purpose for their conference, and they will be forceful in promoting that purpose to the detriment of other aspects. Participants will have a clearer choice among conferences given their needs and the outcomes that they want from a conference.

Physical Settings. Some of the most creative and high-risk investment work in conferencing of the future will be done with the physical setting. Once a purpose for a conference has been isolated, the physical setting that is selected can greatly enhance the atmosphere that helps to determine whether that purpose is achieved.

Colleges and universities have been natural sites for conferences because they are seats of learning and education and because they have conference staffs and faculty for presentations. But, college classrooms are not suited to adult comfort needs; they often lack sleeping and sometimes food facilities, and they are not always located near centers of transportation or nightlife. Colleges and universities have found that they have had to provide more informal meeting places. And, they still offer the best conference prices.

Nevertheless, hotels are now the main hosts to conferences and meetings. They provide for adult comfort needs by carpeting meetings rooms, setting up comfortable chairs in a variety of arrangements, and providing audiovisual accessories, sleeping rooms, and food functions. They are located near major airports and entertainment centers. They will be the centers for conferences of the future, right? Maybe not. While hotels are versatile up to a point, they are not very often specialized. And, as purposes become more narrow, the physical setting will become more important. That is why we are seeing a growing number of conference centers develop specialties based on the purpose of the meeting. Let us visit three.

Elite and Important. The Wingspread Conference Center near Racine, Wisconsin, is located on a beautiful tract of hills, meadows, and river leading to Lake Michigan just a half mile away. The center was designed by Frank Lloyd Wright for the Johnson family of Johnson Wax, which is headquartered in Racine. For many years, Wingspread has served as a conference center for social and educational issues of current import.

The contradictions in the center are apparent as soon as one enters the center: It is the most uncomfortable, inappropriate setting for conferences imaginable, and yet the participants are excited to be there, from the time they arrive to the time they reluctantly leave. Wingspread was not made for conferences, nor was it adapted for them. The ceilings are very low, because the architect was a short man. Persons over six feet five inches should plan on stooping a lot. The rooms are ill-proportioned, and the chairs are not padded. It is very difficult to have good audiovisual presentations. The largest room seats about sixty people, and that is with crowding. There is no room set aside for dining.

Yet, uncomfortable as it is, the architecture is unique and awesome. Around every corner is a piece of sculpture or a painting of significance. The grounds are pleasant, the food is exquisite, and one gets the impression that one is being treated as an important member of an exclusive club. The Wingspread management has fostered that image of elitism and importance in its conferences. Most are held by invitation only, and the topics chosen are of national significance. The staff has turned otherwise unacceptable meeting facilities into a major plus, so that participants feel privileged to be seated in the artistic but wooden chairs, to dip their heads under the low overheads, and to squeeze past others in the narrow halls. Wingspread has achieved national acclaim as a conference center because it has a unique physical surrounding that enhances the perception of elitism and the importance of conference gatherings. The result is that conference participants feel privileged to have attended a small but important meeting on a national issue of great importance in surroundings so special and culturally rich.

Nothing but Training. If you want to learn a job skill fast, efficiently, and thoroughly, the place to go is the Xerox training center just outside Washington, D.C. Located on a campus large enough for a university, the modern-day high-tech facilities are totally geared toward providing training—not learning, not education, but training. Every meeting room has been specially designed to enhance the acquisition of knowledge. Built into the walls is every advanced capability for every kind of audiovisual aid, ranging from slide projector screen to video equipment. The meeting rooms lead into central gathering places where conversation can take place during breaks. The dining and sleeping quarters provide an all-inclusive environment necessary for intensive training. You do not need to leave in order to satisfy any of your basic needs. The result is that thousands of professionals, technicians, and others gain needed job training in the most intensive, efficient manner possible. For Xerox, the purpose was clear, and every aspect of the physical setting was designed with that purpose clearly in mind.

Group Learning, Group Action. In the misty hills of the Great Smokey Mountains forty miles outside Knoxville, Tennessee, is the famous Highlander Education and Research Center. Its founder, Myles Horton, started Highlander more than fifty years ago. Because the purpose of Highlander was to promote human justice and dignity, Highlander has been subject to much harrassment, including legal action to shut it down, suspected arson, and threats against Horton's life. But, Highlander persevered and helped labor unions, civil rights organizations, welfare mothers organizations, and Southern poverty groups in their struggles to make life better. Martin Luther King attended Highlander, and so did Rosa Parks three weeks before the started the Montgomery bus boycott that ignited the civil rights movement of the sixties. But, this famous center, which thousands of people have attended, has only one conference room, no podiums, no microphones, and no wet bars.

The center is built for a maximum of thirty-five people, the largest number that Highlander staff believe can adequately engage in a group discussion. The main conference room is circular, with windows looking over the beautiful mountains that surround it. The room has thirty chairs, many of them rocking chairs, and a fireplace. It was built exclusively for one purpose: group discussion.

Highlander encourages group discussion, group problem solving, group cohesion, solidarity, and group action. And, its physical environment is simply yet wisely developed to encourage that process. Recently, video equipment has been added not for one-way presentations but in order to film participations in discussions and replay them for discussion purposes.

Three sites, three different purposes, three different learning styles—in the future we will see more physical settings tailored exclusively to one kind of learning format and to one kind of purpose.

Subjects. Just because you are a historian does not mean that you should attend a history conference. And, just because you are a plumber does not mean that you would benefit most from a plumbing conference. If you are an adult educator, perhaps you should be attending the history conference or the plumbing conference.

Conference promoters will be seeking to identify new audiences for their events in the future, and participants will have a wider number of conferences to choose from on the basis of subject matter. Strictly institutional conferences will become passé. People will stop attending national association conferences out of loyalty and a desire to support the cause. Attenders will want new learning experiences, a broadening of their knowledge, an exploration of related fields to see what they offer.

If you want to keep on top of your field and be on the creative edge, do this: Attend one new and different conference each year, says James Klassen, a nationally known community educator from Rosemont, Minnesota. This will keep you mentally alert and always discovering.

To encourage and keep new kinds of people coming, conference sponsors will need to rid themselves of the old boys club atmosphere and the closed meetings that typify conferences of the past. They will need to introduce special sessions and other welcoming gestures for newcomers. But, there will be a two-way payoff for conference sponsors who get participants from outside their traditional audience. Newcomers bring another perspective and help to revitalize conferences. The advantages of new blood will benefit both conference participants and conference sponsors.

The High-Tech Conference. With the advent of teleconferencing, computers, and video, will conferences have keynoters who stay home, or will all the participants stay home and just tune in from their living rooms? It seems unlikely that we will soon have successful conferences to which no one comes. In fact, technology will create more human interaction, not less (Naisbitt, 1982).

The computer conference, the teleconference, and the audio conference will all have their place in the future. But, their role will be delegated to two areas: pure information transfer and activities that cannot be accomplished by any other means.

All adult learning will seem to be divided up between two areas: information and education. Technology will make it possible for pure information transfer to be easy, cheap, and less time-consuming. If you want to know how much water to give your houseplants, a software program will be able to tell you. And, few of us will want to sit through an hour and a half of class on Wednesday nights waiting for the instructor to get to gardenias. Instead, we will punch up gardenias on the computer at home whenever we want and get the answer almost instantaneously.

At the same time, issues, attitudes, discussions, and other learning that involves understanding, reactions, and human assistance will flourish even during brownouts, blackouts, and other power shortages. This will be true of conferences and meetings as well. When the subject is pure information transfer, such as the latest technique in welding, data management, or automating the office, conferencing by technology will be enthusiastically received—as soon as the price tag drops. Technology-assisted conferences will offer much better graphics and visual aids, a close-up look at the presenter, and speed in obtaining the information. They will also eliminate having to get there and spending nights away from home, which account for two thirds of the time spent at a conference.

The main obstacle today to such conferencing is the price. Teleconferencing costs a lot of money. But, that will drop. And, it will drop just as the general public becomes acquainted with its advantages and starts to become interested in this way of getting information.

The other aspect of meetings in which technology will play a role is that it is capable of doing things that cannot be done in any other way. For example, public television recently broadcast a live dialogue between a group of American scientists and scientists from the Soviet Union. Because travel between the two countries was extremely restricted in the first half of the eighties, this was the only way in which these scientists could "meet." It certainly was a first for the general public in the United States to be able to hear the comments and views of Soviet scientists. The broadcast was exciting, because it was the only way the meeting could have occurred.

So, technology will have a greater but not a dominating role in conferences of the future. The issue of who will sponsor the teleconferences, audio conferences, and computer conferences of the near future is an interesting one. At this time, it seems likely that there will be only major providers for each technology in a given market area. The costs of becoming involved in the equipment and relay aspects of high-technology learning are so great that only large institutions are getting into it. Even these organizations are losing money now in the main, but they will break even in roughly five years and make money in ten. However, by then they will dominate a given market area and leave little room for organizations that do not have huge resources or a specialized area of expertise.

Presentation Techniques. The American public is starting to get used to video presentations that Steven Spielberg spent $1 million a minute to produce, so who is going to sit still for an overhead projection? The answer is: few of us. Presenters will have to become more sophisticated in their use of audiovisual equipment, including tape recorders, musical instruments, flip charts, slide projectors, video, computer graphics, telephone calls with speaker phones, and a host of other available techniques and aids. Already, these aids are underused at meetings, and often they are being misused. A good audiovisual presentation may take less than a minute, but if it is well done it can be very impressive. In contrast, a presentation technique that has not been mastered and that drags on for minutes creates a very damaging situation for the presenter.

The range of possibilities here is great and exciting. For example, several professional associations are now using so-called poster presentations. Instead of delivering papers, the academics prepare a large poster to convey their ideas. The presenters stand next to their posters in a large hall, and conference participants go around, read the posters, and then ask the presenters questions. This kind of novel approach is much needed, and it will be very welcome at the conference of the future.

Improving Conferences

Those who participate in conferences and meetings will have the most influential say in the efforts to improve conferences. Conferences do not improve by themselves; they improve only when past participants indicate how they can be improved. The conference of the future will be determined by participants as the consumer, not by the sponsor, especially if participants view conferences and meetings as self-directed learning experiences. Participants can control them, or at least they can choose among them. They can "vote" for the kind of conference they want. Enough votes can change a conference format in one year. You can choose to walk away from one conference and into another kind of meeting. Marilyn Hartman of Duke University calls this *feetback*. The most impressive feedback is feetback.

For large organizations, the conference meeting will continue to be important. In the recent past, the annual conference provided as much as 50 percent of an association's income. That figure is rapidly diminishing. But, even today the American Association for Adult and Continuing Education (AAACE) generates 18 percent of its income from its national conference, which is attended by more than 2,000 people. In the future, the annual conference will probably be much less important than it is today in generating income. But, it will be just as important as the organization's premiere event of the year, the showcase by which many people judge the organization's overall effectiveness and vitality. Any national organization has to put its best front forward for the annual conference, and it is this critical publicity and public relations element that will keep conferences improving.

The conference of the future has started already. It is full of potential and rewarding stimulation and interaction. It is also fully dependent on the conference goer. Participants should seek to get their questions answered, meet the people they want to meet, write their own conference agenda, and see that it is accomplished.

86

References

Naisbitt, J. *Megatrends: Ten New Directions Transforming Our Lives.* New York: Warner Books, 1982.

Ries, A., and Trout, J. *Positioning: The Battle for Your Mind.* New York: Warner Books, 1981.

William A. Draves is the director of Learning Resources Network (LERN) in Manhattan, Kansas. He is the author of The Free University and How to Teach Adults.

Not even the best planning can guarantee a successful conference.

Improving Conference Outcomes

Paul J. Ilsley

Conference planning is an important function of scores of associations, professions, and businesses. One primary purpose of conferences is to keep members informed of trends and developments. Another is to promote individual growth through learning. This sourcebook is intended for both planners and consumers of conferences. The emphasis has been placed on association-sponsored conferences; however, other providers can profit from the discussions contained in these chapters. The authors represent a wide variety of perspectives, including those of planner, consumer, and critic. Each provides strategies for enriching conferences through better planning and participation. There is one pervasive theme: to enrich learning in conferences. Every author views conferences as learning opportunities, and each chapter offers a distinct strategy for maximizing conference learning outcomes.

The voice of experience in conference planning comes through clearly in the first three chapters. In Chapter One, Cope presents a tried and tested planning model and explains several useful tools of the trade— structuring committees appropriately, responsibly allocating authority to volunteers—as well as some tips for making conferences financial as well as educational successes. Although Cope's strategy is complex, it can be simply

P. J. Ilsley (Ed.). *Improving Conference Design and Outcomes.* New Directions for Continuing Education, no. 28. San Francisco: Jossey-Bass, December 1985.

summarized: The dedication and efforts of volunteers are essential for the success of a conference.

In Chapter Two, Ratcliff reminds us that a variety of crises can befall even the best conference organizers. Ratcliff's approach is to list major potential problems, especially those that are beyond the control of planners. Since few if any of the problems posed can be anticipated, conference chairpersons must remain flexible and alert. In addition, planners need patience, nerves of steel, and immaculate timing.

Foucar-Szocki brings a distinctive dimension to the discussion in Chapter Three by offering readers some insights into the physical environment, an aspect of successful conferencing that is often neglected. Drawing heavily from the latest research, he traces the effects of variations in room color, air, sound, and space on attentiveness and learning. Moreover, with a keen understanding of the hotel trade, he offers tips optimizing environmental conditions for planners and participants alike.

Chapters Four and Five represent the participant's viewpoint and contain numerous strategies for self-directed conference learning and participation. Although the information in these two chapters may seem primarily to benefit participants, conference planners will find it useful, especially the various checklists and tips for the establishment of volunteer committees. In Chapter Four, Boukouvalas defines conferences as multilevel learning opportunities and persuasively demonstrates why participants profit from predetermining the outcomes of their participation.

In Chapter Five, Meyer. analyzes the unique concerns of conference newcomers. For Meyer, one function of any profession is to bring new members up through the ranks. Newcomers must be involved not only in formal but also in informal activities for this process of integration to occur effectively during conferences. Meyer informs both newcomers and veteran participants of the problems and potential solutions.

The next two chapters supply readers with yet another set of insights into conferences. These authors emphasize special-purpose formats and futuristic concerns. In Chapter Six, Collins discusses the unique opportunities of residential conferences. He argues that residential conferences give participants an opportunity to go beyond mere consumerism toward proactive involvement in such matters as pace and topic of conference. Especially for participants who are dismayed by the frenetic pace and determined efficiency of large conferences, this chapter explains the advantages of planned ambience in residential conferences.

In Chapter Seven, Draves considers future trends in conference planning and consuming. For one thing, conference planning will become a big business, if it has not already, which means that competition to attract participants will become fierce. Moreover, the planning process is likely to become increasingly refined, which suggests that the conference planner of the future will be equipped with a variety of sophisticated planning, marketing, and organizing tools. Despite their allegiance to particular groups and professional associations, consumers will not tolerate unproductive, poorly designed conferences. We need only look to the past for answers to such futuristic problems. Draves cites outstanding examples of conference centers—The Highlander Folk School and Wingspread, to name only two—that have been able to remain responsive to their constituents and pass the test of time.

Effective Planning is Not Enough

Planning a conference is a feat of human engineering because it means coordinating the scores of people who carry out hundreds, even thousands, of tasks, often on a voluntary basis. When this is coupled with the fact that conferences mean many things to many people, it becomes clear that there can be no guarantee of conference success. Not even the best conference planner can predict with any certainty the motivational level of volunteers or the appeal of a conference to participants. It is therefore fair to assert that good planning is necessary but not sufficient for a conference to be a success.

As is true in planning any learning experience, successful conferences depend on matching the expectations of planners with those of participants. Viewed this way, a conference is more than implementation of technical strategy. For example, it is not difficult to imagine a beautifully planned conference that fails to offer anything meaningful to participants. Likewise, conferences that are full of inconvenience and trouble for participants can turn out to be rich learning experiences. The fact is that the best learning experiences are not always planned, because learning is not determined by those who plan it but rather by the learners themselves.

Planning successful conferences requires more than the technical assembly of such program components as public relations, selection of sessions, and evaluation. Books and articles on conference planning typically offer technical guidance and tips; some even provide forms and charts that can be put directly to use. Such material directs attention to efficient models of planning conferences, and it may serve to mitigate aggravation for those who must cope with the enormous pressures of the job. However, efficiency is not enough for successful conferences. Perhaps the best we can expect from perfecting planning strategies is avoiding the crises and pitfalls associated with poorly planned conferences.

Beyond conventional planning lies creating a climate of inquiry. A climate of inquiry is not easy to create. Many factors, including pace, choice, collegiality, quality of interaction, and timing, seem to be controlled less by planners than they are by participants. Such factors evade measurement, and they are therefore difficult to plan. Nevertheless, merely by being mindful of these elusive aspects and by remaining realistic about how much control planners have in their determination, conference planners are well served. The guidelines that follow are meant to foster a spirit of inquiry at conferences:

It is unnecessary to crowd an agenda with activities. Planners can safely assume that people enjoy talking among themselves and that they will do so whenever the opportunity arises.

When participants are included in the determination of conference objectives, the conference is likely to be a more meaningful learning experience.

Although conference planners cannot determine the quality of interaction, they can take measures to break the ice among participants; mixers, "human treasure hunts," opportunities to play, and a general attitude that participants' needs are primary are all useful in this regard.

Participants attend conferences for a variety of reasons. It is safe to assume that one of these reasons is the hope to be challenged intellectually with new material and exciting presentations. Multilevel tracts or an entirely new focus from one year to the next serve a useful purpose in this regard. It is logical to assume that participants prefer a challenging conference to one that is business as usual.

Participants commonly declare that they seek information that they can use on the job when they go back home. Planners can fill this need by offering practical application sessions. However, planners can also go too far in their efforts to accommodate this sentiment, because many participants benefit from discussion of principles and complex topics.

It is easy to underestimate the challenges that participants seek. One implication for conference planners is to schedule a balance of practical workshops and sessions that stimulate thought and new ideas.

Planners can encourage participants to adopt a spirit of inquiry by ensuring that sessions address problematic questions rather than questions that offer easy answers. Although controversial issues can involve risks, they serve to promote discussion and debate among participants.

If conference planners do not have total control over the climate of a conference, it stands to reason that no one does. Yet, it can also be argued that planners and participants have an equal investment in setting the tone. Earlier chapters presented strategies aimed at maximizing participant involvement and at fostering a proactive spirit of learning. The authors have suggested ways of matching participants' expectations with strategies of involvement so that the quality of the experience can be optimized. The onus of responsibility for successful conferences rests both on those who plan and on those who participate.

For Further Inquiry

Most of the literature on conference planning center on nuts-and-bolts tips with respect to design strategies, topic determination, site selection, staffing, facilities, budget design, and evaluation procedures. Materials on these topics often include forms and charts to help planners with the routine of their many responsibilities. One such work is American Society of Association Executives (1979). This booklet is loaded with strategies for establishing the conference planning process. Another example is Burke and Beckhard (1970). Their book provides an overview of the conference planning process and draws heavily on behavior theory in its treatment of how to plan a conference. An edited work, it contains chapters by some of the most respected names in the field. Drain and Oakley (1978) discuss the administration of large conferences and include intricate schemes for organizing them. Hart and Schleicher (1979) provide dozens of charts and planning aids on such matters as conference promotion, budgeting, and exhibits. Loft (1972) presents similar material, but this work is intended for professional organizations, convention bureau personnel, and members of the hotel industry. It achieves its stated purpose of serving as a handbook for convention professionals by offering tips, checklists, and arrangement ideas. Lord (1981) contributes a practitioner's handbook written for business executives that keeps a watchful eye on efficiency. Finally, Nadler and Nadler (1977) have written one of the most comprehensive conference planning books·on the market; their volume covers a remarkable range of conference components.

A second body of material is devoted to the theme of creating a participatory process in the planning and implementation of conferences. The works in this group are based on the premise that interaction of participants from the outset increases conference relevance. Bradford (1976) defines successful conferences in terms of levels of participation. Through small-group process techniques,· communication enhancement, and team building, a desirable level of participation can be achieved. Champlin (1984) presents a process for increasing the level of involvement of particpants in the conference planning process, especially for teacher-educators. Straus (1979) believes that an important purpose of conferences is problem solving, a goal that can be achieved only when participants are active members of the planning process. He adds a cautionary note that large conferences limit participation and defeat the purpose of quality interaction. When participants are involved in the planning process from the beginning, a beneficial snowballing effect occurs that can enhance the quality of discussions as well as outcomes. This (1979) also believes that quality of interaction is an important issue requiring clever manipulation of resources, design strategies, and layout of facilities.

A third body of material, less abundant than the preceding two, considers learning to be the primary goal of conferences. For example, Davis and McCallon (1974) include a primer on adult learning theory and suggest that conference planning can be based on such theory. Elton (1983) makes the case that conferences can be learning and change experiences for participants, but only if participants are prepared in advance, if participants have a hand in determination of objectives, and if the conference itself is planned with very clear objectives. Last, Sork (1984) treats the topic of workshops in a comprehensive edited volume. Workshops are defined as unique learning formats quite different from classes and large conferences that place the emphasis on the participants' quality of learning.

References

American Society of Association Executives. *Making Your Convention More Effective.* Washington, D.C.: American Society of Association Executives, 1979.

Bradford, L. P. *Making Meetings Work: A Guide for Leaders and Group Members.* San Diego, Calif.: University Associates, 1976.

Burke, W. W., and Beckhard, R. (Eds.). *Conference Planning.* (2nd ed.) Washington, D.C.: NTL Institute for Applied Behavioral Science, 1970.

Champlin, J. R. "Conferences: Get Your Money's Worth." *Executive Educator,* 1984, *6* (4), 26, 29.

Davis, N., and McCallon, E. *Planning, Conducting, and Evaluating Workshops.* Austin, Texas: Learning Concepts, 1974.

Drain, R. H., and Oakley, N. *Successful Conference and Convention Planning.* Toronto: McGraw-Hill Ryerson, 1978.

Elton, L. "Conferences: Making a Good Thing Rather Better." *British Journal of Educational Technology,* 1983, *14* (3), 200–215.

Hart, L. B., and Schleicher, J. G. *A Conference and Workshop Planner's Manual.* New York: AMACOM, American Management Associations, 1979.

Loft, V. M. *Convention Liaison Manual.* Washington, D.C.: American Society of Assocation Executives, 1972.

Lord, R. W. *Running Conventions, Conferences, and Meetings.* New York: AMACOM, American Management Associations, 1981.

Nadler, L., and Nadler, Z. *The Conference Book.* Houston: Gulf, 1977.

Sork, T. (Ed.). *Designing and Implementing Effective Workshops.* New Directions for Continuing Education, no. 22. San Francisco: Jossey-Bass, 1984.

Straus, D. "How to Manage a Large Task-Oriented Conference." *Successful Meetings,* 1979, *28* (10), 45–52.

This, L. E. *The Small-Meeting Planner.* (2nd ed.) Houston: Gulf, 1979.

Index

A

Abbot, W. C., 36, 40
Action plan, conference, 6
Adams, F., 69, 75
Adult learning, influences on, 77–79
Agenda, for conference consumption, 48
American Association for Adult and Continuing Education (AAACE), 8, 85
American Society of Association Executives, 91, 92
Approach-approach conflict, 51–52
Armstrong, D., 41
Audiovisual support services subcommittee, responsibilities of, 8

B

Beckhard, R., 91, 92
Bedford, T., 36, 41
Boucouvalas, M., 1, 43–56, 57, 66, 88
Bradford, L. P., 91, 92
Brookfield, S., 55, 56, 63, 67
Brysh-Cooke, C., 53, 56
Budget: administration of, 19–20; concept of, 15; contingency expenses in, 19; detailed, 14–20; evaluation committee and, 19; executive committee and, 18–19; expenditures and, 16–19; gatekeepers of, 17; operations committee and, 17–18; problems, 27–28; and procuring speakers, 7; program committee and, 17; publicity committee and, 18; purchase orders and, 20; purchase requisition system and, 19–20; reducing, 28; reporting, 20; responsibility for establishing, 6; revenues and, 16; staff travel expenses in, 19; vendor invoicing and, 20
Burke, W. W., 91, 92

C

Call for papers, 8
Canter, D., 35, 40
Carlstedt, D. G., 23n
Cell, E., 56
Chairperson, general: and administration of budget, 19–20; attributes needed by, 4; and delegation, 24, 27; illness of, 29–30; and insufficient planning time, 24–25; job change of, 29–30; refereeing by, 26; and resignation of committee chair, 25–26; role of, 4, 6–7
Champlin, J. R., 91, 92
Coffee breaks, 28, 33
Collins, M., 1, 69–75, 88
Committee chairperson: duplication of, duties, 26–27; misunderstanding of, duties, 26–27; resignation of, 25–26
Complaints, 30–31
Concurrent sessions subcommittee, responsibilities of, 7–8
Coordinator. See Chairperson, general
Cope, J. L., 1, 3–21, 87
Copeland, B., 10, 19, 20

D

Daily newsletters subcommittee, responsibilities of, 13
Davis, N., 91, 92
Delegating, importance of, 24
Design, conference: audiences to consider in, 83; features of, 89–90; future, 79–85; improving, 85; influences on, 77–79; presentation techniques in, 84–85; purposes in, 79–80; resources for, 90–92; setting in, 80–83; teleconferencing and, 83–84
Digerness, B., 38, 40
Drain, R. H., 91, 92
Draves, W. A., 1, 39, 40, 77–86, 88, 89

U.S. POSTAL SERVICE

STATEMENT OF OWNERSHIP, MANAGEMENT AND CIRCULATION
(Required by 39 U.S.C. 3685)

1. TITLE OF PUBLICATION: New Directions for Continuing Education

1A. PUBLICATION NO.

2. DATE OF FILING: 10-10-83

3. FREQUENCY OF ISSUE: Quarterly

3A. NO. OF ISSUES PUBLISHED ANNUALLY: 4

3B. ANNUAL SUBSCRIPTION PRICE: $35.00; $25.00

4. COMPLETE MAILING ADDRESS OF KNOWN OFFICE OF PUBLICATION:
433 California St., San Francisco (SF County), CA 94104

5. COMPLETE MAILING ADDRESS OF THE HEADQUARTERS OR GENERAL BUSINESS OFFICES OF THE PUBLISHERS:
433 California St., San Francisco (SF County), CA 94104

6. FULL NAMES AND COMPLETE MAILING ADDRESS OF PUBLISHER, EDITOR, AND MANAGING EDITOR:
PUBLISHER: Jossey-Bass Inc., Publishers, 433 California St., San Francisco, CA 94104
EDITOR: Alan Knox, Teacher Ed. Bldg., Univ of Wisconsin, Madison, WI 53706

7. OWNER:
Jossey-Bass Inc., Publishers, 433 California St., S.F., CA 94104

8. KNOWN BONDHOLDERS, MORTGAGEES, AND OTHER SECURITY HOLDERS:
None

EXTENT AND NATURE OF CIRCULATION	AVERAGE NO. COPIES EACH ISSUE DURING PRECEDING 12 MONTHS	ACTUAL NO. COPIES OF SINGLE ISSUE PUBLISHED NEAREST TO FILING DATE
A. TOTAL NO. COPIES	1388	1361
B. PAID CIRCULATION		
1. SALES THROUGH DEALERS AND CARRIERS	267	89
2. MAIL SUBSCRIPTION	613	668
C. TOTAL PAID CIRCULATION	870	756
D. FREE DISTRIBUTION	94	124
E. TOTAL DISTRIBUTION	974	878
F. COPIES NOT DISTRIBUTED	414	483
G. TOTAL	1388	1361

I certify that the statements made by me above are correct and complete.